The Cooking Book

Fostering Young Children's Learning and Delight

Laura J. Colker

National Association for the Education of Young Children
Washington, DC

Photographs copyright ©:
Donna Dannoff: 13
Janice Langford: 18
Jean-Claude Lejeune: 73
Jonathan A. Meyers: 1
Ken Musen: ix, 11, 72
Marilyn Nolt: 60
BmPorter/Don Franklin: 50, 68

Cover artwork: Sandi Collins
Illustrations: Natalie Klein Cavanagh
Cezanne image: Musee d'Orsay, Paris/Lauros-Giraudon, Paris/SuperStock
Computer clipart: Corel Corporation

Permissions:

Box on page 4 adapted by permission of the publisher from R. DeVries, B. Zan,
C. Hildebrandt, R. Edmiaston, and C. Sales, *Developing Constructivist Early
Childhood Curriculum: Practical Principles and Activities*, (New York: Teachers
College Press), 125–126. Copyright © 2002 by Teachers College, Columbia
University. All rights reserved.

Illustration on page 21 by Jennifer Barrett O'Connell. From *The Creative Curriculum® for Preschool*, by D.T. Dodge, L.J. Colker, and C. Heroman, (Washington, DC:
Teaching Strategies, Inc., 2002), 446. Copyright © 2002 by Teaching Strategies,
Inc. Reprinted with permission.

National Association for the Education of Young Children
1509 16th Street, NW
Washington, DC 20036-1426
202-232-8777 or 800-424-2460
www.naeyc.org

Through its publications program the National Association for the Education of
Young Children (NAEYC) provides a forum for discussion of major issues and
ideas in the early childhood field, with the hope of provoking thought and
promoting professional growth. The views expressed or implied are not necessarily those of the Association.

Carol Copple, publications director. Bry Pollack, senior editor. Malini Dominey,
design and production. Natalie Cavanagh, editorial associate.

Library of Congress Control Number: 2004115557
ISBN: 1-928896-20-0
NAEYC Item: #140

About the Author

Laura J. Colker, Ed.D., is the author or co-author of more than 100 articles, monographs, and books for teachers, caregivers, administrators, and families. She is a co-author of Teaching Strategies' *Creative Curriculum for Preschool*, *Creative Curriculum for Infants & Toddlers*, and *Creative Curriculum for Family Child Care*. Laura is a consultant and teacher trainer for the Department of Defense (DoD) Education Activity's Sure Start and kindergarten programs. She is an intermittent guest editor for *Young Children*, serves as a content consultant to Reading Is Fundamental, and conducts staff development and teaches courses on child development issues worldwide. Her passion is cooking.

To my beloved mother, who gave me "free reign" in the kitchen at age 3,
inspiring a lifelong passion for cooking. And to my wondrous dad,
who made family dinners a forum for learning history,
geography, and groan-inducing puns.

Acknowledgments

Dr. Carol Copple, director of NAEYC's Publications Department, first came up with the idea for this book. Her guidance and laughter made the writing of it a labor of love. I am grateful too to NAEYC's bright and insightful editorial associate, Natalie Cavanagh, who always makes me wonder what I was accomplishing at her age.

This book could not have been possible without the cooperation and support of the many teachers, providers, parents, and grandparents who dutifully tried out the recipes for me, culling the "yucky" ones from the winners. In this respect, I am especially grateful to my colleagues and friends at the Department of Defense Education Activity (DoDEA) who allowed me to build the use of these recipes into my teacher training. Drs. Marc Mossburg and Candace Ransing kindly gave me access to teachers. The wonderful and always festive Bev Erdmann and Jennifer Halley helped me reach the Department of Defense Dependents Schools (DoDDS) teachers in Europe and gently prodded them when needed. Sue Gurley, an unflaggingly supportive administrator, oversaw the use of recipes in DoDDS schools in England and documented the young chefs' work. My deep gratitude goes to preschool and kindergarten teachers Ginger Beavers, Dot Scott, Susan Kilkenny, Janice Langford, Jan Price, Linda Hansen, and Carol Currie-Hannah, who not only made recipe cards and tried the recipes out but also photographed the process for me. Their generous efforts helped validate what is in this book.

On a more personal level, I am indebted to members of my own family and friends who graciously allowed themselves to be coerced into testing recipes. My niece Donna tried several with children at the child care center where she worked, lovingly recording their conversations and photographing the process. My cousin Ken Musen, a professional filmmaker, spent the day at his son Gabe's preschool, photographing the children cooking and eating their culinary treasures. I'm sorry I wasn't able to include Ken's prized photo of a preschooler picking her nose while she vigorously stirs batter with her free hand. I also must thank my friends La Maxine Champion and Monica Vacca. Maxine spent many hours trying out the recipes with her granddaughter Angela, while Monica deftly managed to have her three young sons all cooking these recipes at same time.

I am always appreciative of the wise counsel provided by my close friend and colleague Whit Hayslip. As director of Infant and Preschool Special Education Programs for the L.A. Unified School District, he has made the need for curriculum accessible to all children my mantra. I'm equally indebted to Diane Dodge and Cate Heroman, my co-authors on the fourth edition of *The Creative Curriculum*, who helped me refine my thoughts as I wrote a new cooking chapter in 2002. In addition, I am grateful to Heather Benson, of Reading Is Fundamental (RIF), who enthusiastically tracked down recommended titles of food-related children's books.

Finally, I must acknowledge my dear friend Bob Cerullo, who lent me use of his magnificent beach house so I could work on this book in an atmosphere brimming with beauty and inspiration.

My unending appreciation goes to all the teachers and young children who let me into their classrooms so I could share my love of cooking with them.

Contents

Preface

I come from a family that reveres food. We don't just eat to live and live to eat; we regard cooking and eating as our inspirational fount. Food has always nourished us body and soul.

When I grew up, family meals were sacrosanct. We have always been a family that spent each meal discussing the where and what of our next one. A highlight of our worldwide travels has been the delights of food. I clearly remember as a child in nursery school listening raptly as my mother read a letter from my dad, who was working in Australia. He wrote to us not of Sydney's magnificent harbor or of Tasmania's unique koalas and echidnas, but of the country's sweet, succulent strawberries. Forty years later when I traveled to Australia for the first time, I immediately set out to taste those berries.

My passion for cooking was born in this atmosphere. Delighting my family with my very own creations was a source of unending pride, and sharing my mother's kitchen with her multiplied my excitement. Even as a little girl of 3 or 4, I knew that I was onto something special.

When I started working with children some 30 years ago, I naturally expanded my love of cooking to include cooking with children. At first, I just wanted to share my enthusiasm with the children. My motivation was no deeper than a feeling that something so meaningful to me as a young child would bring similar pleasure to other young children.

As I matured as an educator, I realized that a great many educational and research-based reasons supported why cooking should be a natural part of the preschool and kindergarten curricula. When Diane Dodge and I began to plan the third edition of *The Creative Curriculum for Early Childhood* in the late 1980s (Dodge & Colker 1992), I successfully lobbied to include cooking as an interest area, putting it on a par with blocks, dramatic play, and the reading area.

I have long viewed cooking as a motivational gateway to learning. Young, curious children—who are constantly investigating the world's mysteries—are naturally drawn to cooking. They take pleasure in watching popcorn kernels pop open and transform into a yummy snack. They are awed at how batter in a muffin tin solidifies as it bakes and produces an aroma that arouses all of their senses. They are mesmerized at how yeast proofing in a bowl bubbles like a volcano, causing dough to rise.

As I myself realized as an independence-seeking young child, cooking is one of the few opportunities young children have to participate in adult activities. In dramatic play, children whip up a pretend treat for their baby dolls. In cooking, they actually make their own snack. Cooking develops children's sense of competence as they see a task through to completion, just as their parents do.

As I have observed over the years, early childhood educators can involve children in cooking and food-related activities in many different ways. Typically, teachers bring children together for a special cooking project. This endeavor may be to make a pizza or bake pretzels for snack. Or children might make a dish typical of a holiday, for example, latkes for a Hanukkah celebration. Birthdays, likewise, can be an occasion for baking cupcakes to make the day special for the birthday child. On other occasions, teachers may cook with children to reinforce a book that has been read aloud, for example, Dr. Seuss's *Green Eggs and Ham* or the folk story *Stone Soup*.

Sometimes, too, children "cook" for purposes other than eating. For example, making playdough scented with powdered fruit drink can be an exciting art activity. Mixing cornstarch and water to form the strange, unstable substance known as *oobleck* is a fascinating hands-on science lesson.

Cooking activities like these have rightly found a place in many early childhood programs. Some teachers try to make group cooking projects a weekly event. This effort is a start, but it falls far short of the full learning potential of cooking. This book is about making cooking a daily experience and a fundamental part of a curriculum for young children.

In this book I also argue for taking cooking beyond the whole group context. Just as children in the block area or the art center work individually, in pairs, together with a teacher or parent volunteer, or in small groups, they can participate in cooking activities in all of these configurations. Each of these ways of experiencing cooking has its particular value, as we will see.

Cooking as a daily learning activity can benefit any type of program—school, center, or family child care home. Over the past 20 years, I have trained thousands of teachers in making cooking an integral part of their programs. Sometimes the idea is viewed skeptically at first, as "one more thing I have to do." But I can say that every teacher I have trained who has adopted this approach has reported back to me that cooking with children has improved program quality and has helped children to learn concepts and skills. Learning academic concepts in a functional context assists many children in making connections to literacy, math, and science skills that were difficult for them to master in the abstract.

For a time, rumors circulated that Howard Gardner was going to add cooking to his list of multiple intelligences. Although I was disappointed that this addition never came to pass, I will continue always to describe cooking ability as a type of intelligence. It is an area in which children can shine and excel. It is also a domain that teachers can use to teach socioemotional, cognitive, physical, and literacy skills as well as to foster children's creativity and self-expression. My firm belief is that cooking— like block building, reading, and the arts—should be an integral part of every preschool and kindergarten program.

—*Laura J. Colker*

PART ONE

Food for
Thought

1

Getting Started

When starting up a cooking program with young children, it is important to keep the "big picture" in mind. How do you envision your program? Do you want to make cooking a regular part of your curriculum? Do you want children to use the cooking area for preparing and eating their morning and afternoon snacks? Do you want children to help decide what they are going to make? How can you ensure that children will be both supervised and independent while cooking? Will all children in your program participate in cooking activities? How will you accommodate children's differing skill levels?

These are some of the important questions that teachers need to reflect on before starting a cooking program. The answers to these questions will guide your teaching practices. The first part of this chapter highlights some of the initial considerations for implementing a cooking program. Next, the chapter presents some approaches to using the cooking area that will enable children to maximize their learning experiences.

Developmental readiness

By age 3, most children find cooking activities appealing. Nevertheless, not every child will be ready to start making recipes—at least not without being introduced to the process and having a chance to experiment a bit.

Just as children naturally explore books, sand, playdough, and other materials by using all of their senses, they initially explore cooking opportunities in the same way. You may find that some children in your program are so intrigued with cooking materials that they can't focus on doing any actual cooking. Zan, Edmiaston, and Sales relate the following example of this sort of cooking experience in a Head Start classroom.

> Near the beginning of the year, Christie . . . and her teaching partner Gwen . . . were anxious to begin cooking and chose [a] muffin recipe. . . . At group time Christie demonstrated how to make a muffin. She showed the children (ages 3 and 4 years) how to measure by leveling off their measuring spoons with a wooden tongue depressor and how to measure and add water and oil without spilling. During the following few days, she sat at the cooking table during activity time, helping each child who chose to make a muffin. After witnessing successful muffin making and appropriate use of the materials, she decided to allow the children to make muffins independently, with adults nearby to supervise the use of the microwave.
>
> Checking in later to see how the muffin making was progressing, she noted that few children were really measuring. Most children were just dumping ingredients in the bowl. Christie explained to Gwen that these were beginning steps and that experimentation was necessary. She predicted that when the children saw the results—inedible goo—they would begin to follow the recipe. However, a short time later a classroom volunteer called her attention back to the cooking table where one child was holding the bottle of oil upside down and squeezing. The child watched, fascinated, while oil ran everywhere. (2002, 125–26)

What went wrong and what could these teachers have done to avoid the problem? After they saw what was happening, the teachers recognized that the children needed time to explore and experience the ingredients and utensils without worrying about making a recipe. So before setting up a cooking activity again, they put flour in a clean sand table and gave the children measuring spoons, measuring cups, and sifters. The children poured, dumped, and sifted the flour. They also made pretend cakes and muffins. They experimented with adding water to the flour, observing that the more water they added, the thinner the flour paste became. Once the children's experimental play started progressing to a higher level, the teachers decided that it was time to retry the cooking experience. This time, the children were ready to make muffins.

You may find that some children will need to go through a similar "messing about" stage with any significantly new type of cooking material, just as they do when they first encounter a new art material. So be prepared to allow this exploratory period before you introduce any new type of cooking experience to young children.

Basic cooking techniques

After the children have had many opportunities to explore, take time to introduce them to basic cooking techniques like pouring and mixing. This progression fosters children's success in cooking and also assures you that children will be using implements properly—and safely. Teach each technique in two steps:

First, introduce children to the technique by modeling how it is done and by verbally walking children through the process. This step works best either with individual children or with small groups of two to four children. Let children observe you several times.

Next, give children practice doing the technique either with you or on their own while you watch, comment, and encourage them. After practicing several times, most preschoolers and kindergarten-age children can master basic cooking techniques.

At this point, you can be confident in letting children do many cooking maneuvers—those that pose no safety hazards—on their own. Occasionally, you will want to check back with the children to determine whether they are encountering problems and to lend your support. When children are using techniques that have potential for accidents—cooking with heat, cutting with sharp knives, grating, or grinding, for example—adult supervision is a must, no matter how proficient children are (see Chapter 3, PUTTING SAFETY AND HEALTH FIRST).

As you are introducing cooking techniques, look for natural teaching opportunities and raise questions to further children's learning:

- How else could we remove eggshells from the hardboiled eggs if we didn't want to use our hands?

- What happens to the cream when we beat it with a whisk?

- How is measuring flour using a glass measuring cup different from using a metal measuring cup?

- How can we keep the lemon seeds from falling into the juice when using a reamer?

- Can you think of anything else we could use a huller for besides pulling out strawberry stems?

The table **Appropriate Ages and Activities for Mastering Cooking Techniques** can be used as a guide in presenting techniques to children.

You may choose to introduce these basic techniques in isolation or as part of beginning cooking experiences. Just be sure that you closely supervise the children's mastery of techniques before moving forward. If you have children of varying ages in your program, make sure that younger children are proficient in the lower-level skills before introducing a higher-level skill. Not all children need to perform all skills. Take your cues from the children's development. Once children are skilled in the basic cooking techniques and are aware of health and safety requirements, then they are ready for cooking adventures.

Appropriate Ages and Activities for Mastering Cooking Techniques

Technique	Age	Activities for Practicing the Technique
Stirring/mixing	2–3	Mixing pudding, combining ingredients in a bowl
Shaking	2–3	Shaking container of salt, making butter out of cream
Spreading	2–3	Putting peanut butter or cream cheese on crackers
Scrubbing	2–3	Washing vegetables with a brush
Greasing	2–3	Spreading butter or shortening on a cookie sheet
Tearing/breaking/snapping	2–3	Tearing lettuce, breaking off ends of green beans
Dipping	2–3	Placing bread in an egg mixture for French toast
Kneading	2–3	Making bread dough
Dredging	2–3	Rolling chicken pieces in flour
Using basic cooking gadgets (whisks, basters, spatulas, strainers, colanders, cookie cutters)	2–3	Stirring batter, straining liquid, cutting shapes out of cheese
Wrapping	3	Rolling lettuce leaves around filling, putting aluminum foil around a baking potato
Pouring	3	Pouring glasses of milk or juice, filling blenders or colanders
Rolling (with a rolling pin or hands)	3	Making cookie dough, meatballs
Measuring	3–4	Filling measuring cups and spoons
Peeling with hands	3–4	Taking off eggshells, husking corn
Cutting soft foods	3–4	Slicing bananas, boiled carrots, or cooked potatoes
Using nonelectric appliances (food grinder, chopper, eggbeater, juicer/reamer)—with adult supervision	3–4	Making peanut butter, lemonade
Cracking eggs	4	Tapping eggs at center and using hands to separate shell over a bowl
Using electric appliances (blender, mixer, electric frying pan/wok)—with adult supervision	4	Making smoothies, batter, sautéing
Cutting with a knife—with adult supervision	4	Cutting cheese, hard-boiled eggs, bread
Grating—with adult supervision	4	Grating apples for applesauce, carrots for salad
Mashing	4	Using masher or fork on boiled foods, bananas
Coring, hulling, pitting—with adult supervision	4–5	Preparing strawberries, cherries, apples for eating
Peeling with a vegetable peeler	4–5	Removing skins from potatoes, carrots
Cracking nuts	4–5	Using a hammer or nutcracker to open nuts

Meaningful cooking experiences for children

The following sections present some of the major ways that teachers and providers can involve children in meaningful cooking experiences. These approaches include using specific areas (e.g., snack centers, tasting tables) and providing opportunities for individual children and for various-size groups of children.

Snack centers

Perhaps the best way to begin a cooking program is to start with snacks. All young children need to have them, and all teachers offer them. What is different in the approach described here is that snacks are part of an ongoing cooking program rather than simply an eating break for the children. By incorporating snacks into your cooking program, you take advantage of a natural bridge for teaching children about cooking. Moreover, by making their own snacks, children become involved in the learning opportunities that cooking provides.

Snacks in the form of a cooking activity make the most sense when programs already have family-style dining, experiences offered for break-fast, lunch, or both. Family-style dining, where everyone sits and eats at the same time, provides wonderful advantages for social growth that should be part of every early childhood program. If you already serve one or both meals family style, you can then handle snack time in a different way that further enhances your program. Instead of devoting 15–20 minutes each morning and afternoon to a food break, why not make these snack times an independent activity in the cooking area that is built into children's "choice" time?

Independent snacking has a number of obvious advantages. Besides the learning benefits that children receive by preparing their own snacks, the opportunity to decide when and how much to eat is another big plus for children. By taking personal responsibility for their own snack, children can begin to develop a healthy approach to eating.

Snack centers are the preferred way of most teachers to incorporate independent snacking into the daily schedule. The following steps show how to use the snack center approach:

- Add snack time as an option during the daily choice time. The time at which children must have a snack is not designated; rather, children can visit the cooking area at any time during this period and help themselves to a snack. The cooking area is treated as any other center in your program—as a learning choice for children.

- Designate a section of the cooking center for snack. In most cases, the eating table can serve this purpose. Make the table attractive by, for instance, covering it with a brightly colored tablecloth and putting out a vase of fresh flowers. Some teachers like to hang a sign over the snack table, designating the area "Kids' Cafe" or "Snack Shack."

- Put out all of the needed ingredients for the snack on the table or a nearby counter.

- Prepare a daily snack menu, with suggested serving portions. Use both words and pictures—"Today's Snack: 2 graham crackers, 8 raisins[1], and water (as much as you want)."

- Adopt the rule that the number of children having snack at one time can't be more than the number of chairs at the table (typically four to six).

- Make sure that children maintain a clean space. They should know to wash their hands before and after handling foods and to clean up after eating so the next diners will have a clean place to have snack.

- Set up a system to handle the traffic flow. When the snack table is full, other children who want to eat can "write" their names on a sign-up sheet to reserve a turn. (Teachers should record separately which children have and have not eaten snack in a given day to ensure each child gets enough to eat.)

- Remind children about the snack choice. Ten minutes before choice time ends, announce that all children who have not yet visited the snack center but who would like something to eat should head toward the "Kids' Cafe." Teachers can also extend individual invitations to children who have been absorbed in play and might not have thought about their need for eating.

Tasting tables

Another easy way to foster children's involvement in food exploration and cooking activities is to set up a tasting table in the cooking area. As the name implies, a tasting table offers children the opportunity to explore interesting foods that may be new or unfamiliar to them. What is

---

[1] Because of their potential as a choking hazard, raisins should be served only to children who are 4 years old or older.

new to a child, of course, depends on that child's individual background. So include variety in your choices, and try to introduce foods that children from the various cultures in your program might be served at home. Also include exotic (or exotic to preschoolers and kindergartners) choices such as crystallized ginger, raw fennel, or mascarpone. Their names alone will be fun to learn. You may get a "Yuck!" response now and then, but surprisingly, many young children respond positively to tastes that adults assume are too sophisticated for them. Also, try introducing the same foods in different physical states so children can observe material changes and also decide what forms of the same ingredient taste better to them. For example, you might offer children yogurt and frozen yogurt to compare and contrast or a cold cheese sandwich and a grilled cheese sandwich to taste.

In addition to providing individual foods for tasting, try introducing two or three foods at a time so children can make comparisons. You might try offering different foods from one of the groups in the USDA Food Pyramid, for example, a trio of fruits like apple, mango, and banana. Or you might try foods of similar shape such as Brussels sprouts and cabbage or foods of similar colored flesh such as papaya and cooked sweet potato. Alternatively, you might pick a tasting theme such as foods that grow underground or foods that cool you off on a hot day. While tasting foods with similar names—for example, cooked spaghetti pasta and cooked spaghetti squash—children can note how these are alike and how they differ.

As children taste different foods, encourage them to describe the experiences and to compare and contrast foods by asking questions of this sort:

- How does it taste? Can you think of other foods that have a similar taste?
- What does it smell like? Can you think of other foods that have a similar smell?
- Is it easy to chew? Does the food stick to your mouth?
- How does it feel on your tongue? Does it taste different after you swallow it?
- Why do you think they call this squash "spaghetti squash"?
- How are the fruits alike? How are they different?
- Do you think this food would be a healthy choice to eat? Why is that?

Using a tasting table is also a good way to engage children in mastering some of the steps of the scientific method. Children can hypothesize what foods will taste like based on looks and smells and then can compare their predictions with reality. You can lead children in making graphs about their discoveries and in charting who liked what. The tasting table can be a lively, enjoyable place for budding scientists.

Children cooking on their own

Independent cooking is one of the best uses of the classroom cooking area. Just as children benefit from reading a book by themselves, doing a puzzle on their own, or painting independently, they thrive when engaging in a cooking activity on their own. Remember that children cooking independently means no adults second-guessing their every move. For the children's safety and your peace of mind, be sure to offer children who are cooking independently those recipes that do not involve heat or equipment such as grinders, blenders, or mixers that need supervision. A number of the recipes in the RECIPES-FOR-ONE section included in Part Two suit this purpose well, including the following:

> *No-Sting Honey Bee Snack*
> *Happy Trails Mix*
> *Cheese Shapies*
> *Ants on a Log (or Marching Raisins)*
> *Fish Swimming Upstream*
> *Full of Baloney Roll-Ups*
> *Ice Cream in a Bag*
> *Underwater Jell-O*

In setting up the cooking area for children to use independently during choice time, try the following approach:

• Select recipes that can be concluded within the amount of time scheduled for children's choice activities. Typically, allow 45 minutes to 1 hour, if the child spends the full amount of time in the cooking area. Offer children recipes to do on their own that are ones they have previously done successfully. This strategy will help ensure a positive cooking experience.

• Have all of the ingredients for the chosen recipes available for children to use independently. If ingredients need to be cold or at room temperature, make sure that they are at the appropriate temperature.

• Make sure that safe supplies for cleaning up are stocked and available for children to get at themselves. You want young chefs not only to be able to cook independently but also to clean up on their own.

- Let children know that an adult is always available to assist them if they feel that they need help. In addition, check on the chefs occasionally to see how they are doing.

- When interacting with children, offer an occasional question or comment that helps children learn new vocabulary or make a connection to a math or science concept. For example, "What did you have to do to the Jell-O powder to make it harden?" or "How many teaspoons of water did you need to add to get one tablespoon?"

- Encourage children to regularly document their cooking experiences by making a drawing, dictating the experience to you, or having you photograph their creation. Let them decide how and when they document their efforts.

Cooking together with one or two children

Although independent cooking is something that should occur regularly in all programs, you can enhance the learning process by being there with children as they cook. Obviously, you or another adult can't always be positioned in the cooking area, so you should reserve these sessions for times when you can make the cooking experience a teaching time.

Your working hand in hand with one or two children enriches the cooking experience for them. It also allows children to use implements and appliances (such as blenders, sharp knives, electric frying pans) that they can't use on their own. This means that children have a much broader repertoire of recipes from which to select. Two children can elect to work on recipes independently or together on the same recipe. The teacher is there to provide both supervision and expertise.

Your interacting with one or two children as they cook expands their learning. Through your conversations, observations, and questions, you can support and extend children's learning. The following strategies enhance this process.

Plan out the learning connections you hope to make in this cooking experience. Before you start cooking, think about your learning goals for the children and reflect on how the cooking experience might help to achieve these objectives. For example, for promoting fine-motor skills, think about how squeezing lemons will develop small muscles in the hand. To encourage children to make predictions, you might ask them, "How do you think the honey will change the taste of the lemon juice?" To solve problems, ask children, "How can we keep the honey from forming a big lump in the bottom of the pitcher?" Or if you are concentrating on measurement, you might ask, "How will we know when we have 1 cup of honey?" Pinpointing important concepts and prompting with sample questions introduces learning concepts in a natural, thoughtful way.

Describe what you see children doing. "You mixed the wet ingredients with the dry ingredients and now all of the ingredients are wet." When you verbally describe what you have observed children doing, you call attention to details they might not have noticed. Moreover, as you describe their actions, children mentally revisit what they have done. Reinforcement of this sort focuses children on the steps and processes they are learning. In addition, providing verbal descriptions is a natural way to introduce new vocabulary words that are so useful in cooking and in general language development.

Encourage children to reflect on what they have done and to put their ideas into words. "You've been beating those eggs for a long time. What's happening to them?" As children think about what they are doing and seeing, they develop greater awareness of the scientific changes and cause-effect relationships that are inherent in cooking.

Use questions and comments to probe more deeply. In particular, use questions and comments that spur children to make connections: "Why do you think the avocado turned brown? Remember what we did to make the bananas stop turning color? Do you think the same thing would help the avocados?"

Use open-ended questions that encourage children to do the following:

- Make comparisons. "The yogurt and the sour cream look alike, but how are they different?"
- Apply past knowledge. "The raisins got bigger when we soaked them in water. What do you think will happen to the prunes if we soak them? How about grapes?"
- Make predictions. "What do you suppose will happen to the cheese on the nachos if we put them in the microwave?"
- Devise creative solutions. "What can we do with the orange rinds after we've squeezed the juice out of them?"

- Solve problems. "We know that the muffin batter will rise when it bakes, so how high should we fill the muffin tins?"
- Become more aware of their own thinking (metacognition). "What made you think of using the whisk to stir with?" "How will you know that the milk is about to boil?"

Cooking with a small group of children

Often, teachers will want to do group cooking experiences. In the past, many teachers tried doing cooking projects with the whole class. Their efforts were rarely successful. Children ended up watching their classmates and waiting a very long time before they got to do something. Frustration usually overtook enthusiasm.

Most teachers will tell you that cooking with groups of four to six children is a far more effective approach to group cooking activities. If teachers want to give everyone a chance to participate, they can repeat the activity three or four times. In small groups, everyone has a chance to make the recipe. The children are actively participating, not just standing around watching others cook. In addition, small groups are an excellent venue for teaching teamwork, for fostering social negotiation and positive conflict resolution, and for promoting learning.

Probably the most effective way of managing small-group cooking activities is to designate a staff member or parent volunteer to be present in the cooking center. Let children know that the small-group cooking activity is an option for choice time ("Ms. Donna will be helping to make *Lickin' Good Lemonade*") and remind them that only the number of children for whom there are chairs can work at one time. When one group of children finish, another group of children can take their places.

In the small-group context, you can use nearly any recipe in Part Two. The SMALL GROUP RECIPES and the ART AND SCIENCE RECIPES are designed to be made by groups of four to six. You can also use the RECIPES-FOR-ONE in this context, with each child at the table making his own version of the same recipe. The advantage of this method is that each child gets to make an entire recipe herself.

She can also compare and contrast her product with those of her classmates.

Whether you work with several children on one group effort or on their individual efforts to make the same dish, assemble all of the ingredients, equipment, and appliances the children will use in one place. Go over each step in the recipe with the children, reviewing and asking questions to make sure that they understand what is in store. Have the children wash their hands and don their aprons or smocks. Then add, "Enjoy yourselves!"

During the cooking activity, follow the same suggestions as provided earlier for cooking together with one or two children. Plan ahead to determine the learning objectives you want to address. Describe for the children what you see happening. Encourage them to make predictions, reflect on their actions, and describe what they are doing. Then, through open-ended questioning, engage children in making comparisons and categorizations. Guide them to apply past knowledge to new situations where they can make predictions and solve problems. Help them to be creative, active learners.

The following transcript recounts how one teacher, Ms. Donna, introduced *Lickin' Good Lemonade* (see p. 120 for recipe) to a small group of 4- and 5-year-olds:

> **Ms. Donna:** (*reviewing the ingredients with the children*) "What kinds of tastes are we working with this time?"
>
> **Several children:** "Sweet! Sour!"
>
> **Tristan:** "I love sour."
>
> **Ms. Donna:** "Why do you like sour tastes, Tristan?"
>
> **Tristan:** "They feel good on my tongue."
>
> **Ms. Donna:** "What are some things that taste sour?"
>
> **Cheyenne:** "I love lemons."
>
> **Kayla:** "I like sweet."
>
> **Ms. Donna:** "What are some sweet foods?"
>
> **Niu-Niu:** "Sugar."
>
> **Ms. Donna:** "Yes. Sugar is what makes food sweet. Can you think of some foods that taste sweet because they have sugar in them?"
>
> **Kayla:** Candy is sweet.
>
> **Ms. Donna:** "Yes, that's about as sweet as a food can get."
>
> **Tristan:** "Are sweet potatoes sweet?"

Ms. Donna: "Yes, they are a bit sweet. That's good thinking, Tristan. Why do you think we're mixing the very sweet with the very sour?"

Cheyenne: "So it gets yummy."

Ms. Donna then demonstrates how the reamer works and explains how the holes filter out the seeds. Each child is given half a lemon to juice.

Ms. Donna: "How does it feel when you squeeze it?"

Niu-Niu: "Hard. And squishy."

Ms. Donna: (*holding up a lemon*) "What do you see when we're done squeezing the lemon?"

Several children: "Nothing!"

Tristan: "The lemons are so empty!"

Niu-Niu: (*pointing to the small amount of juice in the measuring cup*) "When is it going to be a lot, a lot of lemonade?"

Ms. Donna: "Soon. After we mix in the water and honey." (*Cheyenne takes a turn at stirring in the honey.*) "OK, Honey, mix up the honey!"

The children squeal with delight.

Ms. Donna: "How does it smell?"

Kayla: "Mmmm. Smells like honey! And sour!"

Once the lemonade is finished, Ms. Donna has each child pour a cup of the lemonade.

Ms. Donna: "OK. Let's take a sip. So, how does it taste?"

All: "Good." "Mmmm."

Cheyenne: "Yummy for my tummy."

The children excitedly drink their lemonade.

Extending children's learning

Once a cooking activity is over and the resulting dish is eaten, don't let the children forget about what they have experienced and learned. Reinforcing the concepts and learning that came up in the cooking activity increases children's retention of this knowledge and their ability to apply it later. Think about the many ways that you can build on what children have done in the cooking center. Try to think of activities that will engage children and keep them wanting to learn more.

Consider the recipe for *Accordion Tomato,* which consists of half of a tomato with mozzarella cheese slices inserted into it, as an example (see p. 87). You probably won't do all of the following things for one recipe, but they illustrate the kinds of things you might consider to extend children's learning.

- Find out or ask what the children liked best about doing this recipe. Was there a part they didn't enjoy? Would they change this recipe if they were to make *Accordion Tomato* again?

- Have the children analyze which of the Food Pyramid's food groups tomato and cheese belong to. Are they healthy foods? What vitamins do they contain? How do they help our bodies grow?

- Invite the children to think about what they would serve along with tomatoes and cheese to make a balanced meal.

- Discuss how the recipe got its name. Some children may get interested in accordions, especially if you share with them one or more books on the subject. In the library, you can find books such as *The Man Who Played Accordion Music* or *Hector the Accordion-Nosed Dog.* You may want to play some accordion music for interested children or place CDs and tapes in the listening area. One album that many children enjoy is *Planet Squeezebox: Accordion Music from around the World* (1995, on Ellipsis Arts). The science of how the accordion works is another area for exploration.

- Have children explore other objects in the world around them that, like the tomato in the recipe, resemble an accordion. They can fold paper strips accordion style and make puppets and pop-up collages.

- Have children use other ingredients to make different types of accordion salads—for example, cheddar cheese slices in an apple or mango slices in a peach.

- Plan a field trip to a neighborhood tomato farm, perhaps even one that grows tomatoes hydroponically in greenhouses by using nutrient solutions (water and fertilizers) rather than soil.

- Plant some tomatoes in the class or school garden. If the children are interested in growing tomatoes inside, or if it is not feasible to have an outdoor garden, search for information on hydroponic tomatoes on the Internet. When the tomatoes ripen, use them for making the *Accordion Tomato* recipe for snack.

- Consider making homemade mozzarella cheese—which is delicious and is a natural opportunity for learning science (see pp. 118–19). Because the process takes a while and is complicated, it is best done when an interested parent volunteer can participate. Children will learn that cooking tools need to be sterilized every time they are put into a milk mixture so bacteria won't change the flavor of the cheese. They will also learn that the famous "curds and whey" they know about from the "Little Miss Muffet" rhyme is a natural part of making cheese. Curds and whey are formed when milk is separated out into lumps (curds) and liquid (whey). The enzyme rennet, which can be readily purchased from cheese supply stores, speeds up the separation process. Children will also learn new vocabulary words such as *sterilize*, *spiral*, *crosshatch*, and *diagonal*.

- Enter the completed cheese recipe on the computer, as part of a class cookbook project. Then, encourage children to illustrate how they made mozzarella, incorporating their art into the book. You might also take digital photos to document the cooking steps. Families will enjoy having a copy of the class cookbook so they can make these same recipes at home.

- Encourage children to re-create the cooking activity in the dramatic play area. Children can pretend they are running a restaurant where *Accordion Tomato* is served. When the dramatic play area is stocked with appropriate utensils (pans, spoons, dishes) and clothing (aprons, chef's

---

Encourage Children to Create Their Own Recipes

When children have become familiar with a few basic recipes, they can begin to suggest variations. For example, in one classroom where children had many experiences making banana yogurt shakes in a blender, the children decided they wanted to make a different type of shake. They had a class discussion in which they talked about several options and decided on peaches. One child suggested that they try ice cream rather than yogurt in the shakes; so they made a shopping list for the teacher, and the next day they made their peach shakes.

Sometimes children are simply curious about what will happen when they mix certain ingredients together. The results of these experiments are usually not very successful from a culinary standpoint. This introduces the controversial subject of wasting food. For some people and some cultures, using food for activities other than meals is considered a violation of a primary value. If this is the case, then allowing children to experiment with combining and cooking different ingredients may not be appropriate (except when the result is likely to be edible). However, if wasting some food in the interest of education is acceptable, then allowing children to experiment with cooking different foods in different combinations can be fruitful.

hat), children will be encouraged to enact various scenes. Don't forget to put some of the recipes in the play area, too.

Three final words are important to remember for enhancing children's learning about and through cooking: document, document, document. Documenting children's efforts should be an integral part of everything that takes place in the program. Take photos of the children cooking and engage them in helping you to identify and write captions for what is going on in the pictures. Interview children and record their thoughts about what they were doing and thinking during each step of the process. The photos shown below, for example, are from a series documenting a small group of 4-year-old children making the *Long on Shortcake* recipe (see p. 96 for recipe).

Dionte is scooping fruit cocktail onto biscuit halves in a mini muffin tin.

They taste so good!

In reading this chapter, you have begun to think about how to incorporate cooking into your curriculum. Now we turn to setting up the environment, which is essential in ensuring successful cooking experiences for young children.

2

Setting Up to Cook

With square footage at a premium in most early childhood classrooms, teachers may be reluctant to devote the space needed for cooking in an already crowded classroom. They may prefer to store cooking supplies in a cupboard and bring them out on an as-needed basis. But if cooking is to be a daily learning activity, it has to be treated with the same respect given to all learning centers. Most teachers wouldn't think of storing blocks or books in a cupboard and bringing them out only for special events. Cooking, too, needs to have its own center in the classroom.

When selecting an area of your classroom for cooking, approach the task as you would when setting up any center. Think about the requirements of the activity area. Ideally, the cooking center should be

- near a sink, so children can wash their hands before and after handling foods and have access to water when it is needed in cooking;
- in a spot where there are electrical outlets, so blenders and other electrical appliances can be used;
- out of the way of traffic patterns, so children can cook undisturbed.

In addition, avoid using an otherwise quiet area of the room such as near the listening or reading area. Cooking tends to generate lots of excitement and voices rise; cooking utensils and appliances can be noisy, too. Spaces next to the art, sand, or water area are good choices because children tend to be loud when playing in those locations. These areas could also share a common sink. Just make sure that the cooking area is located far enough away so sand or paint won't get in the food.

Once you have pinpointed where the cooking area in your classroom will be, you'll need to define the area visually and physically. Low, open shelving (24–30 inches in height) makes an ideal boundary. The shelves can then be used to store cooking equipment such as a colander or muffin tins that children can easily reach.

In the center of your chosen cooking area, place one or two child-size tables with seating for four to six children. Should you have room for two tables, one can be used for food preparation and one for eating. This arrangement allows you to keep the eating table looking festive—perhaps covered with a red and white checked tablecloth and a vase of fresh flowers. More likely, though, the room will allow for just one table that serves both functions.

Often, children are preparing a recipe other than that day's snack—for example, lemonade to serve a guest or gelatin to put in the refrigerator and examine later. In this situation, children's snacks can be placed on a counter or perhaps on top of the shelves used as the room divider. Or if the table is large enough, the cooks can work on one side, and the children who are snacking can fix and eat their snacks on the other side.

Beyond these basics, you will need a pegboard to hang utensils and potholders as well as perhaps a clothes tree on which to hang aprons. On the walls at the children's eye level, you can place posters such as the **Food Guide Pyramid for Young Children** (see p. 38), posters featuring international foods, or even posters featuring fine art prints (such as Wayne Thiebaud's whimsical cakes). Children's artwork depicting their cooking experiences and creations are also great to display. Here or elsewhere in the room you can also post photos documenting the children's cooking activities, with captions expressing the children's explanations of what the photos have captured.

The illustration on the following page depicts a well-thought-out cooking center. This design incorporates these features:

- The focal point of the area is the child-size table with surrounding chairs. This table grouping serves as both a workstation and an eating area.
- Open shelving defines the space.
- Kitchen utensils and supplies are arranged on the shelves.
- Labeled contact-paper shapes define where items are stored.
- A counter at the children's elbow level is pushed against the wall to make use of the electrical outlets.
- Laminated pictographic recipe cards are posted where children can consult them.
- A pegboard for hanging measuring cups, spoons, aprons, and potholders is within the children's reach.

Cooking Center

Children wear aprons to protect their clothing.

Safe cooking tools are within the children's reach.

Recipe cards guide the cooking activities. It is set up for self-serve snack so children can prepare and eat their snack whenever they wish.

Water is close at hand to assist both cooking activities and cleanup.

• Mops and sponges used for cleanup are stored near the sink.

One final point on selecting an area for cooking: If you are in a center- or school-based program, avoid using the facility's kitchen. At first glance, it might seem that having access to a real kitchen would be the ideal setup, but it isn't. First of all, the tables, chairs, and counters are not child-size. Second, it requires constant supervision, which prevents children from ever being able to use the area independently. Third, it is removed from the classroom, which defeats the purpose of classroom learning centers. You can make use of the kitchen's refrigerator for storage or its oven for baking, but don't regard it as your classroom cooking center.

The situation is different in family child care. If you care for children in your home, you can and should make use of your family kitchen. Capitalizing on the home environment for the children's activities is fundamental to family child care. Just as writing and art may take place on a coffee table in the living room or at the dining room table, cooking takes place in the kitchen, not in a separately designed learning center.

Home kitchens need not pose the same dangers that center kitchens do. In the family child care setting, you can childproof your kitchen in ways that institutional settings cannot. Moreover, family child care programs have fewer children for the provider to supervise, and they may include older children who can lend additional guidance to the younger ones.

At the same time, using your home's kitchen does require preparation and vigilance on your part. Chapter 3, Putting Safety and Health First, features a complete listing of safety measures that will make the home kitchen safe for cooking with children. In brief, they include doing the following:

- Childproofing the kitchen. Electrical outlets and cords need to be made safe. Potentially toxic cleaning supplies have to be stored in locked cupboards. Knives and other sharp tools need to be out of reach.

- Storing flammable items such as potholders, dishtowels, paper towels, and napkins away from burners to prevent fires.

- Making accommodations for the height of the sink. A step stool or low bench can be used to help children reach the sink.

- Supervising constantly. Young children should never be left alone in the kitchen. If babies or toddlers are a part of the family child care grouping, they should be placed in high chairs or infant chairs where they can taste foods and observe the action, but not disrupt the older chefs.

Using the family kitchen with children in family child care homes is different from setting up a cooking learning center in a classroom, but the benefits of the cooking experiences are the same.

Stocking a cooking center

It is easy to get carried away with gadgets and appliances, but try to resist. Too many items can be confusing to children, and costly as well. Begin by matching your inventory to the first recipes you are going to introduce. As children become comfortable with the equipment and learn to handle items safely, introduce new ones gradually. When selecting items for your inventory, consider the following points:

- Always select real preparation items over "child" or toy ones. Real implements not only make the experience more authentic but also are safer to use. Fewer accidents occur when children are taught to use real knives correctly than when they attempt to cut with a plastic "pretend" chef's knife. The same goes for eggbeaters, graters, and the like.

Outdoor Cooking

Many cooking activities can also be enjoyed outdoors. This is especially true if a picnic is also planned. Cooking outdoors is quite different an experience from cooking in the confines of the kitchen. This less controlled environment can present both challenges and benefits as children adapt to wind, sunlight, and curious insects.

Introduce children to new cooking tools appropriate for outdoor use, such as a grill, hibachi, or outdoor hearth. You may even wish to build a solar cooker that uses the sun's rays to heat food (information about solar cookers is readily available on the Internet). The sun's energy can also be used directly, such as when making sun-dried tomatoes. Here's how:

Start with Roma tomatoes from your class garden or farmer's market. (They are the meatiest of tomatoes and carry less water.) Cut them in half lengthwise, and carefully place the halves, skin side down, on a framed nylon or plastic screen. Put a cheesecloth cover over the screen to protect the tomatoes from dirt and insects. Raise the cheesecloth off the tomatoes slightly with bamboo skewers. Then place the screen outside in the sun. Count on a few days of drying. Be sure to bring the tomato screens indoors each evening, once the sun goes down.

Children can also use the sun's power to make sun tea:

Fill a large glass jar with water and add several herbal tea bags and maybe a spice or two (cloves or fennel seeds give off a refreshing scent). Cap the jar and set it in a hot, sunny spot. After several hours, check to see if the tea is dark. When it is, add ice and let everyone sip their homemade iced tea.

Other recipes in this book, such as *Sun Clay* (p. 130), *It's for the Birds* (p. 142), and *Clean Mud* (p. 137), are ideally done outdoors. Likewise, the bubble-making recipes found in ART AND SCIENCE RECIPES are intended for outside play. Nothing is more fun on a windy day than blowing billowy bubbles that reflect the colors of the rainbow. Use plastic strawberry containers, empty eyeglass frames, or the plastic circles that hold a six-pack of soda together to make interesting bubble wands for *Basic Bubbles, Monster Bubbles*, or *Fancy Schmancy Bubbles* (all p. 141). For a special treat, fill a small wading pool with *Monster Bubbles* solution and place a hula hoop into the pool. A barefoot child can step into the hula hoop and pull it up. The end result is a bubble with a child in the middle!

Finally, don't forget to set up recycling areas outside, where children can separate out glass, aluminum, plastic, and paper wastes from outdoor cooking projects and play.

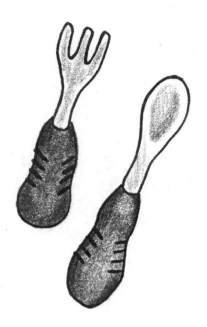

- Unlike implements, serving pieces intended for children are best, because a child-size bowl or pitcher is a replicate of the adult-size item. Being able to pour from a child-size pitcher or lift an item with a child-size tongs makes the experience more manageable for young children.
- In general, select nonbreakable items that won't shatter if accidentally dropped. In the past, the only exception teachers made to this rule was the use of Pyrex measuring cups, so children could observe what was being measured. Today, however, clear measuring cups that are made of hard plastic are readily available.
- Look for utensils with soft grip handles. Good Grips brand utensils, for example, were developed for adults with arthritic hands; they work equally well for the small hands of young cooks.

The following list outlines a basic inventory for a classroom cooking area. At first glance, the length of this list may seem overwhelming. But think about picking and choosing those materials that you can use in beginning cooking activities with children. As children become more experienced, work your way up to a fully stocked cooking area. Many teachers find it helpful to start out with equipment they will need for preparing basic snacks and one or two other types of activities, such as cooking with an electric wok and baking.

Cooking and Baking Equipment

baking/cookie sheet or jellyroll pan
baking/cake pans (various sizes)
muffin tins (regular and miniature sizes)
frying pan
loaf pan
roasting pan
pizza pan
saucepans with lids (various sizes)
large pot
cooling rack

Appliances

electric wok or electric frying pan
blender
hand mixer
grinder
toaster oven
microwave oven
stovetop burners and oven
refrigerator or cooler

Utensils and Gadgets

mixing bowls

measuring cups

measuring spoons

spreaders or butter knives

serrated knives

chef's knives

candy thermometer

timer

can opener

colander

eggbeater

funnel

ladle

masher or ricer

wooden spoons

slotted spoon

rubber spatulas

silicone spatulas (for use with
high heat)

nylon or silicone turner

wooden cutting board

cooking shears or scissors

sifter

strainer

wire whisk

tongs

jar opener

peeler or corer

graters (for cheese, for nutmeg)

huller

melon baller or scoop

mortar and pestle

citrus reamer or juicer

rolling pin

ruler

cookie/biscuit cutters

pastry brush

pastry bag, coupler, and tips

Supplies

paper towels

aluminum foil

plastic wrap

plastic resealable bags
(various sizes)

dishtowel

cheesecloth

cupcake/muffin liners (paper)

waxed paper or cooking
parchment

oven mitts or potholders

aprons

dishpan and drainer

dishwashing and cleaning
supplies

Serving Utensils

plates

platter

cereal bowls

child-size flatware

napkins

placemats

glasses or tumblers

pitchers

metal spoons and forks

Safety Equipment

kitchen fire extinguisher

box of baking soda

first-aid kit

Storage and display

The first rule of thumb in placing items in your cooking center is an obvious one: Any items that pose a safety danger to children need to be stored out of the children's reach—including electrical appliances, knives, and sharp objects like graters and corers.

With the remaining items, you'll want to take the opposite approach. The key to storing these safe items is to make them as accessible to children as possible. Open shelving and pegboards are especially effective. As in other areas of the classroom, display picture and written labels where items are stored. For items hung on pegboards, use shape labels so children can match items to their shapes. And, as always, use print labels functionally to give children the information they need. For example, you would label a colander, but not the table or chairs.

In addition, consider grouping items by function to increase children's independent use of the cooking center—for instance, place mixing items together in one place, baking items together, cleaning supplies together, and so forth. If you run out of space, extend the cooking area through the use of "themed" boxes. Similar to the way you might keep prop boxes for various dramatic play themes, all of the specialized equipment children would need for making a cake or a pizza can be stored in separate boxes. Supplies can be retrieved as needed.

If you are using your home kitchen for cooking with children in family child care, you may wish to consider setting up some drawers at lower levels for the children to use. You can put utensils and safe cooking supplies in these drawers, easily within children's reach. Picture and word labels indicating where these gadgets go will help children to both use them independently and return them when they are clean.

Adapting the cooking center for children with special needs

Children with disabilities, like all children, respond positively to cooking experiences. There is no reason to exclude any child—even those with severe disabilities—from cooking activities. By making accommodations, all children can experience what Irma Rombauer (1931) long ago termed the "joy of cooking."

In order to provide effective support, start by looking at the child's current level of development. How is that child functioning physically, socially, emotionally, cognitively, and communicatively? Children with disabilities show a wider range in their development across these areas than children who are typically developing. It is essential that staff take time to observe children with special needs and together plan for the children's involvement.

This planning process can lead to decisions about how best to support individual children during cooking activities. Some children may need changes in the physical environment, such as using spoons with broader handles or bowls that can be secured to the table, while others may need more opportunities to feel, explore, and experiment. More adult modeling and repetition, or perhaps a reduction in the noise and distractions, might be what is called for. Many children with special needs will need more time to complete activities and may need to work in smaller groups. Some may need more verbal cues and still others may need more adult support and individual attention. Whatever the form of the support, as the child's level of participation increases, staff should observe and respond to the changing needs of the child. This is the same process we use for all children as we help them maximize learning in the early childhood classroom.

Depending on a child's disability, you can make adjustments to either the physical environment or the equipment to ensure that all children have a successful cooking experience. Patti Gould and Joyce Sullivan (1999) offer concrete suggestions for adapting learning centers to meet the needs of children with specific types of disabilities in their book *The Inclusive Early Childhood Classroom.* In addition, the following suggestions review some steps you can take to make cooking more accessible to children with disabilities.

• Make use of adaptive cups, utensils, and dishes. Suction cups provide a stable base for both eating and cooking bowls as well as dishes. Dycem, a rubberized nonslip material, can also be placed under bowls and dishes to prevent slides and spills. In addition, bowls and plates are available with one side built up, which makes scooping easier.

• Consider using weighted utensils to give the child more sensory feedback and to improve coordination.

• Think about playing calm background music, which can be relaxing to easily distractible children.

• Use a tray or placemat to define a child's eating or work space.

When a child with a disability comes to a program with specific learning objectives indicated on an Individualized Education Program (IEP), it is important for staff to come together to think about how these objectives can be addressed within the classroom activities. Cooking activities provide a rich context for working on many of the objectives that are commonly included in the IEPs of young children. These activities are filled with opportunities for addressing language, motor, social/emotional, and cognitive needs. By working together, staff can develop specific strategies for using the cooking activities to help children meet their individual goals.

Parents are essential partners in the development of these individual strategies. Creating an open relationship with regular opportunities for communication and sharing will greatly increase the program's ability to effectively meet the child's needs.

The successful inclusion of children with disabilities in cooking activities is built on this strong foundation of focused observation, ongoing planning, and decision making. It is not dependent on single right answers or highly technical techniques. When programs are committed to including children with disabilities and they make time for this kind of observation and planning, *all* classroom activities, including cooking, become richer learning opportunities for *all* children.

As we have seen, considerations of the physical environment for cooking are essential in setting the stage for meaningful learning experiences with children. Once the cooking center is laid out and stocked, you are almost ready to invite the children in to cook. But first, you need to consider the important points that are discussed in the next chapter, PUTTING SAFETY AND HEALTH FIRST.

3

Putting Safety and Health First

Teachers who shy away from cooking with children tend to do so because of the potential for accidents. Envisioning worst-case scenarios of cut fingers and classroom fires, they figure the safest practice is to avoid putting children "in harm's way" altogether. With knowledge and confidence, however, teachers can create safe and supportive learning environments. Teachers who are apprehensive or who have never engaged children in cooking before can start slowly, beginning with simple activities and basic concepts.

Safety measures to prevent accidents

The best way to avoid accidents is to take some basic preventive measures:

- Keep potentially dangerous equipment (knives, corers, graters, grinders, and all electrical appliances) out of children's reach; stored in a cupboard, for example. Bring them out only when children will be cooking under adult supervision.

- Keep knives sharp; dull knives are more dangerous because their blades drag instead of cutting quickly, efficiently, and cleanly. Drag causes the user to press harder and to lose control.

- Stock the cooking area with potholders that are thick enough to keep the heat from penetrating. Pot grips made of silicone are highly recommended because they are both waterproof and heatproof. Provide insulated utensils for stirring hot mixtures.

- Store potholders, dishtowels, and aprons away from burners and other sources of heat.

- Make use of only nontoxic cleaning agents and store them in locked cupboards or closets.
- Make sure that electrical outlets are not overloaded and are covered with safety caps when not in use. Make sure that your hands, the plugs, and the sockets are dry before plugging in appliances. Keep cords out of children's reach when appliances are being used.
- To prevent burns, make sure water from your hot tap is set to not exceed 120 degrees Fahrenheit. To check the temperature, turn on the hot water tap and let it run until it reaches its hottest; fill a glass with water, and use a candy thermometer to register the temperature.
- Keep a box of baking soda on the counter and a fire extinguisher as well as a first-aid kit nearby—just in case. Make sure supervising adults know basic first aid, including how to handle choking and burns.

Educating children about cooking safety

Equally important as preparing the environment is educating children to use the environment and materials safely. Education is most crucial in dealing safely with fires, heat, ovens and stoves, and knives. In general, accidents with appliances typically occur either because children are too short to reach them or because children have not been properly trained in their correct usage.

Fire safety

Make sure that children know what to do in the event of a fire. If a fire occurs while cooking, it needs to be extinguished with baking soda; water may make it spread. If the fire is in a pan, throw the lid on top to smother the fire. If children's clothes catch on fire, they should know to "Stop, Drop, and Roll": Stop running, drop to the floor, roll to put out the flames.

Heat safety

Children need to understand that hot pot handles and boiling liquids can burn them. Hot drinks and soups can scald even after sitting for 20–30 minutes. Make sure that children follow these heat safety measures:

- They use only wooden spoons or heat-resistant silicone spatulas to stir or turn contents in hot pots and pans, because metal utensils get very hot.

- When using a stovetop, they turn pot handles toward the center or back of the stove, so the handles do not overheat and are not accidentally pushed or bumped.
- When taking lids off heated pots or pans, they lift the lid such that any escaping steam won't burn their face.
- They put water only into empty, cool pots or pans. Water poured into a hot pan will sizzle—and also will ruin the pan.

To reinforce important safety rules, discuss them often and have children role-play the safety precautions. The following scenario shows how one teacher went about reinforcing heat safety education in his preschool classroom.

At morning circle, Mr. Avera, a preschool teacher, announced to the group that he and several students would be performing a skit for the other children on cooking safety. Anyone who wanted to watch the skit was welcome to join them in the housekeeping area.

As Mr. Avera and Tyler, Bev, and Jennifer assembled in front of the stove in the housekeeping area, other children sat on the floor and in beanbag chairs. Mr. Avera announced to the audience that he would be reading the story *Stone Soup* and that while he read, Tyler would demonstrate how to make the soup.

As Mr. Avera read from the book, Tyler playacted adding ingredients to the large saucepan on the stove. Very dramatically, Tyler turned the pot so the handle was sticking out front. Next, everyone watched as Bev came over to see what Tyler was doing. As she peered over the pot, she "accidentally" knocked into the handle, causing the pot and its contents to come pouring out all over her. "Ow!" Bev cried out in her loudest voice. "I'm burned." "Oh no," cried Tyler and Mr. Avera. "We've got to get her to the hospital." On cue at the word *hospital*, Jennifer came to Bev's aid, dressed in scrubs with a stethoscope. "I can get you better, Bev," said Dr. Jennifer. "But this is one accident that didn't have to happen."

After the actors took their bows, Mr. Avera led the audience in a discussion on how this accident could have been prevented. The group discussion focused on the need to keep pot handles turned inward on a stovetop to prevent accidental bumps like the one Bev had experienced.

If a burn occurs, first aid needs to be applied at once. First aid for slight (first-degree) burns involves flushing the reddened area with cool running water and loosely applying moist dressings and a bandage. For more serious, deeper (second- and third-degree) burns, loosely apply dry dressings and a bandage. Do not use water on deep burns because it may increase the risk of shock. Of course, serious burns require immediate medical attention once first aid has been applied.

Oven safety

The Ohio State University Extension Service (1992) has developed a public awareness campaign on appliance safety for children, known as PAUSE (Parents Appliance Use and Safety Exchange) With Children.

PAUSE With Children offers the following advice for using microwaves safely with children:

- Do not attempt to operate the microwave with the door open or when the oven is empty.
- Show children how to cook foods in the microwave. Foods like pizza and popcorn need special packaging designed specifically for this purpose.
- Caution children that stored up heat may cause burns.
- Show children which dishes are safe to use in a microwave oven.
- Use potholders to remove cooked foods from the oven.
- Open covers or plastic wrap away from the user to avoid steam burns.
- Never heat containers that have small openings, such as syrup bottles.
- Pierce nonporous skins or membranes of foods to prevent steam buildup and bursting.
- Stir liquids before heating them to avoid eruptions when containers are removed from the microwave oven.
- Do not boil eggs in the shell in the microwave; they will explode.
- Remove wire twist-ties from paper or plastic packages before placing packages in the microwave oven; the metal in the ties can cause a fire.
- Use only thermometers specifically designed for use in a microwave oven.
- Do not overcook foods.
- If materials inside the microwave oven ignite, *keep the oven door closed*. Turn off the power immediately by turning off the oven and unplugging the power cord.

PAUSE With Children also recommends teaching children the following about using a gas or electric stove:

- Wear proper clothing. Loose-fitting or baggy sleeves can catch fire when a child reaches across a burner.
- Use dry potholders. Wet potholders can cause burns from steam.
- Do not leave burners unattended.
- Watch fat and oil closely so they do not become too hot and catch on fire.

- Never touch heating elements, because they may be very hot despite looking cool.
- Do not set bowls, utensils, towels, etc., near electric units or gas burners where they could catch fire.

Knife safety

Young children can learn to use real knives safely. Begin by giving children a butter knife or table knife with which they can strengthen their coordination skills. Provide opportunities for children to practice cutting and spreading soft foods with the knife, for example, slicing a banana or putting cream cheese on a cracker. At the same time, let children use kitchen shears to snip parsley and get used to working with a sharp edge. When children can handle both a butter knife and kitchen shears with ease and competence, then introduce them to using a small paring knife or one with a serrated edge. These knives can do most cooking tasks. Make sure children know, however, that knives in any form are to be used only under the supervision of an adult.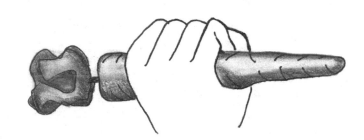

According to chef Lynn Fredericks (1999), adults need to keep in mind two main rules when using knives while cooking with children: (1) teach children to keep the noncutting hand safe, and (2) as noted earlier, use only sharp knives. In instructing children, show them how to hold the knife by the handle and how to use their other hand to hold the food that is to be cut. Children need to learn to tuck the tips of the fingers under their knuckles into a clawlike position when holding the food to be cut. This hand positioning is important because cuts tend to happen to the hand holding the food, not the hand doing the cutting. Also, from the start, get children in the habit of using a cutting board.

To your good health

Health concerns are just as important as safety issues when it comes to cooking. In fact, health problems are more likely to occur than accidents are. Early childhood classrooms can be breeding grounds for germs. Just look around your classroom; at any given moment, one of your children is likely to be sneezing or coughing. The fact that these open mouths and runny noses will be around food makes it imperative that you be vigilant about hygiene and sanitation practices.

The most important thing that everyone in your classroom can do to promote good health is to wash their hands well and frequently. If a child is sneezing or coughing, she needs to direct the sneeze or cough toward her shoulder (not her elbow as once advised) or the floor and then wash her hands. Even children and adults without colds or infections need to be frequent hand washers. Before and after anyone handles foods, his or her hands must be washed.

Many teachers recommend hanging a picture chart of proper handwashing procedures right above the sink. In many ways, these charts are like recipe charts; steps are broken down and depicted in both picture and written form. Laminating the poster will make it last longer.

Disinfection is likewise important to preventing the spread of disease. Tabletops and counters need to be disinfected daily with a freshly made bleach solution of ¼ cup of household bleach to 1 gallon of water (or 1 tablespoon of bleach to 1 quart of water). After cleaning surfaces with detergent and rinsing them with water, you should spray surfaces with the bleach solution until they glisten. The solution either can be allowed to air dry or can be wiped dry with paper towels after two minutes.

In addition to these basic hygiene and sanitation procedures, you should also observe the following procedures to make sure that cooking activities take place without incident:

- Use wooden cutting boards. After many years of debate over the virtues of plastic versus wooden cutting boards, wood is the definitive winner. According to microbiologists at the University of Wisconsin–Madison Food Research Institute, wood wicks moisture from debris, a characteristic that can kill microorganisms (Andersen 1993).

- Wash all fruits and vegetables before handling.

Five Steps to Healthy Handwashing

1. Wash under running water that drains—not in a stoppered sink or container.

2. Use liquid soap to make a lather.

3. Rub hands together for 10 seconds (20 seconds is even better). Children can sing a song (such as the ABC song) that you have timed out as lasting 10–20 seconds to mark the appropriate time.

4. Dry hands with a paper towel. When finished, use the paper towel to turn off the faucet.

5. Apply hand lotion. (Dry, cracked skin traps germs.)

Adapted from S.S. Aronson, with P.M. Spahr, *Healthy Young Children: A Manual for Programs* (Washington,DC: NAEYC, 2002), 18.

- Wash tops of cans before use.
- Never reuse a spoon that has been used for tasting.
- Keep hot foods hot and cold foods cold to prevent bacterial growth. Don't let perishable foods stand outside the refrigerator for more than two hours.
- Cook foods thoroughly at the appropriate temperature.
- Don't allow nibbling during cooking, as much fun as that may seem. Foods that may become safe once cooked, such as chopped vegetables, can be hazardous popped into a young child's mouth during prep. Plus, it's unsanitary—just think of handling raw eggs then sticking the same fingers into the cream cheese for a taste!

Before you begin any cooking activities, it is vitally important to know whether children have any food allergies or intolerances. For example, it is not unusual for young children to be allergic to peanuts or to be lactose intolerant. Other common irritants to children are eggs (especially the whites), tree nuts such as pecans or walnuts, fish and shellfish, soy, and wheat. Be sure to consult the children's records and talk with their families before undertaking any cooking activities. The goal is to safeguard children from harm, and at the same time enable them to fully participate in cooking activities. One solution is to substitute for problem ingredients. (For more on substitutions for health as well as cultural and religious reasons, see **Finding a Good Substitute** on p. 75.)

Finally, if you teach young preschoolers or toddlers, you need to be alert to potential choking hazards. The box opposite lists common foods that are choking hazards and ways to make them safer. By age 4, most children have physically developed to the point that they usually can eat these foods safely. Older preschoolers tend to chew foods better, and their larger upper airways do not block as easily as those of younger children. Never-

---

**Foods That Are Choking Hazards
(and Ways to Make Them Safe)**

Be careful of foods that are
- Round—for example, whole grapes or hard candy
- Firm—for example, hot dogs, nuts and seeds, chunks of meat, and raw carrots
- Stringy—for example, celery sticks or citrus fruits
- Sticky—for example, peanut butter, marshmallows, raisins, or caramels
- Likely to be eaten by the handful—for example, popcorn, pretzels, or chips

You can make foods safer by
- Slicing hot dogs and grapes lengthwise
- Parboiling carrots until slightly soft and then cutting them into sticks
- Spreading peanut butter thinly
- Cutting meat into small pieces
- Chopping nuts and seeds finely
- Pitting fruits
- Removing the pith from citrus fruits
- Shredding hard vegetables

theless, it is always good practice to know what to do should a child of any age suddenly choke. Even if licensing doesn't require it, all teachers and providers would be well served by taking a one-day child CPR course.[1] With this certification, you will know how to administer the Heimlich maneuver to young children if a choking emergency occurs. In addition, post emergency health and safety phone numbers nearby. When emergencies arise, you need to be able to respond immediately.

Preparing for safety and health mishaps is your insurance policy. Chances are you won't ever need to deal with an emergency. However, should one occur, you need to be ready.

Food literacy

Beyond the clear priority of preventing accidents and illness, teachers also promote children's health by focusing on good nutrition and eating habits. We know from research that children develop food habits at a very young age (Debord & Hetzler 1996; Parker-Pope 2003; Barbour 2004). For example, when young children are rewarded with sweets, they develop a tendency to reach for a candy bar or a pint of ice cream to celebrate a happy event or to ward off the blues. These food habits contribute to what has been termed an epidemic incidence of childhood obesity (Troiano et al. 1995), the early onset of Type 2 diabetes, high blood pressure, and the weakening of bones. In later life, these bad eating habits learned in childhood are correlated with heart disease, liver disease, and forms of cancer.

The rapidly rising rate of childhood obesity in the United States is a topic of much concern. Indeed, approximately 20 percent of young children ages 2–5 and 30 percent of children ages 6–11 in the United States are now overweight (CDC 2004). These percentages are four times the rate of 25 years ago (AOA 2002). Although increased TV viewing, video games, and other sedentary activities contribute, there is no denying that food behaviors play a causal role in this trend. One factor that has been linked to poor food choices is the increasing decline in eating together as a family. Studies in the United States, Ireland, Taiwan, and Finland have found that children who ate dinners with their family members ate more fruits, vegetables, and dairy foods than children who didn't dine with their families (Eneli & Crum 2004). According to a story in the *Wall Street Journal*, "The lesson is that when parents are present at the table, the meal is more likely to be healthful and the kids are more likely to eat it" (Parker-Pope 2003).

---

[1] Local chapters of the American Red Cross continually sponsor CPR sessions. See www.redcross.org for information.

Teachers who cook with children are in an ideal position to help children form good eating behaviors and make wise food choices. Eating wisely is what food literacy is all about.

A useful tool to support you in teaching children to make healthy food choices is the Food Guide Pyramid for Young Children: A Daily Guide for 2- to 6-Year-Olds, from the U.S. Department of Agriculture (USDA) first released in 1999. This guide (shown on p. 38) is based on actual food patterns of young children that were analyzed from 1992 to 1998 by the Center for Nutrition Policy and Promotion (CNPP), part of the USDA's Food, Nutrition, and Consumer Services office. The Center found that the foods that children ages 2–6 eat most often are somewhat different from foods eaten by older children and adults. For example, more of young children's Meat Group servings come from less-healthy ground beef and luncheon meats than from high-nutrient fish. Young children are also more likely than adults to eat ready-to-eat cereals, which tend to contain high amounts of sugar. In addition, compared with older children and adults, young children are less likely to eat salads and raw vegetables and more likely to eat cooked green beans, which tend to lose vitamins in the cooking. They are also more likely to drink fruit juice (which has high sugar content) than to eat whole fruit. (For more information about the children's Food Guide Pyramid, see the CNPP website at www.usda.gov/cnpp.)

Overall, the USDA found that most young children are not consuming a sufficiently varied, well-balanced diet. Even earlier, the American Dietetic Association (1993) had concluded that most young children's diets are too high in fat and too low in fiber. Further, estimates suggest that at the very most only 20 percent of young children eat five or more servings of fruits and vegetables a day; for Latino children, the estimate is 6.8 percent (Basch, Zybert, & Shea 1994).

The Food Guide Pyramid for Young Children thus reflects children's eating patterns in the context of their nutritional needs. Guidance is given on how many servings of each food group in the Pyramid young children need in light of what they already tend to eat—and not eat.

The five food groups defined in the Food Pyramid are distinguished by the nutrients they provide. The Grain Group, for example, provides primarily carbohydrates, iron, and thiamin. Being at the base of the pyramid, grains represent the largest dietary need for preschoolers and kindergartners. At the top are Fats and Sweets, which ought to be eaten sparingly, though not entirely eliminated from a child's diet. In between are the Milk, Meat, Fruit, and Vegetable Groups containing foods that children need to have in substantial amounts. These groups provide

FOOD Guide PYRAMID

for Young Children

A Daily Guide for 2- to 6-Year-Olds

Fats & Sweets — Eat LESS

MILK Group 2 servings

MEAT Group 2 servings

VEGETABLE Group 3 servings

FRUIT Group 2 servings

GRAIN Group 6 servings

Center for Nutrition Policy and Promotion
U.S. Department of Agriculture
Program Aid 1651
January 2000

USDA is an equal opportunity provider and employer.

FOOD IS FUN and learning about food is fun, too. Eating foods from the Food Guide Pyramid and being physically active will help you grow healthy and strong.

WHAT COUNTS AS ONE SERVING?

GRAIN GROUP
1 slice bread
1/2 cup of cooked rice or pasta
1/2 cup of cooked cereal
1 ounce of ready-to-eat cereal

VEGETABLE GROUP
1/2 cup of chopped raw or cooked vegetables
1 cup of raw leafy vegetables

FRUIT GROUP
1 piece of fruit or melon wedge
3/4 cup of juice
1/2 cup of canned fruit
1/4 cup of dried fruit

MILK GROUP
1 cup of milk or yogurt
2 ounces of cheese

MEAT GROUP
2 to 3 ounces of cooked lean meat, poultry, or fish.

1/2 cup of cooked dry beans, or 1 egg counts as 1 ounce of lean meat. 2 tablespoons of peanut butter count as 1 ounce of meat.

FATS AND SWEETS
Limit calories from these.

Four- to 6-year-olds can eat these serving sizes. Offer 2- to 3-year-olds less, except for milk.
Two- to 6-year-old children need a total of 2 servings from the milk group each day.

Source: U.S. Department of Agriculture Center for Nutrition Policy and Promotion.

The Cooking Book

additional carbohydrates as well as protein, vitamins such as A and C, and minerals such as calcium, iron, and zinc.

In reading the Food Pyramid, bear in mind the wide variation in what constitutes a "serving." A serving of bread, for example, will vary according to children's ages and metabolisms. An older, active preschooler will typically eat one slice of bread as a serving. Most 3-year-olds, however, typically require only half a slice of bread as an average serving size. Consequently, do not consider the serving sizes listed in the Pyramid as exact amounts. Rather, let children determine what constitutes a serving size for them. The number of servings is what should remain constant for all preschoolers and kindergartners. At their ages, it is much more important that they eat a variety of foods rather than an exact measurement of one food.

For children with small appetites, teachers should consider the following recommendations:

• Do not insist that children eat when they are not hungry.
• Keep healthy snacks available between regularly scheduled meals.
• Offer more energy-enhancing foods such as peanut butter, cheese, and higher-fat yogurt and milk than might ordinarily be served.

In addition to a wide variety of foods, all young children should have six to eight 4–6-oz. servings of water daily. Because the percentage of water in a child's body is higher than in an adult, children can become quickly dehydrated. Adults need to offer children water several times a day, even when it is available on demand.

Appendix A presents recommended daily food choices for children in preschool and kindergarten. The chart explains how many servings of each food group young children ought to have. The emphasis is on eating a variety of foods and making smart food choices. **Appendix B** offers planning menus for morning and afternoon snacks. Using these suggestions as a guide, you can help children learn to recognize healthy or unhealthy food choices.

Children, with teachers' support, can learn to use the Food Pyramid Guide to plan a healthy diet. When children make a recipe, help them relate what they are making and serving to the Food Pyramid so they can understand the relationship between what they eat and good health. Analyzing the recipes can also help children make wise food choices and, perhaps, may lead to forgoing a sweet treat for a healthier one.

Most of the recipes in this book represent more than one food group. Analyzing the ingredients in these recipes can help children understand the importance of eating a variety of foods from all of the food groups

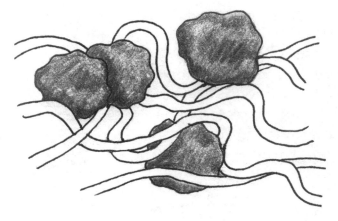

each day. Consider the recipe *Cheese-Louise Meatballs* (see p. 88 in RECIPES-FOR-ONE), for example. Using the Food Pyramid as a reference, you can help children match the ingredients to the food groups they represent so children can see how having a serving of these meatballs will help them meet their daily food requirements. The table below can guide teachers in discussing this relationship with children.

As shown, if a child were to prepare and eat all of the recipe himself, he would be well on his way to eating a balanced diet for the day. He would have met most of his daily requirements for the Meat and Milk Groups and would have started on his Grain Group requirements. During the rest of the day, he'll need to concentrate on fruits and vegetables and more grains. And, if he's very active—like most children his age—he can have some sweets and fats in moderation.

Making children aware of the nutritional value of the foods they eat empowers them to start taking personal responsibility for their own well-being. This extends not just to eating but to all healthy practices. For example, we know from research that when children in their preschool and kindergarten years develop a sense of personal responsibility, they develop the heightened self-esteem that makes them more likely to resist peer pressure to try drugs when they are older (Partnership for a Drug-Free America 2004).

Try to make the link between nutrition and cooking each time a child uses a recipe. One way of graphically making this link is to create your

Daily Food Requirements in a Serving of *Cheese Louise Meatballs*		
Ingredient	Food Group	Servings
½ lb. ground turkey	Meat	3
¼ teaspoon salt	N/A	N/A
dash of pepper	N/A	N/A
¼ lb. Swiss cheese	Milk	2
1 egg	Meat	½
¼ cup Product 19 cereal	Grain	⅓

own Food Pyramid game. When a child selects a recipe to cook, supply him with a laminated Food Pyramid chart on which you have glued Velcro dots to each food grouping. Then provide the child with laminated food cutouts (that have Velcro backings) of each ingredient in the recipe. Let the child match the ingredients to the appropriate food groups. Once the foods have been matched to their areas on the Pyramid, you can then discuss the health merits of the recipe. While you wouldn't want to do this with every cooking activity, do it often enough so that children regularly begin making food-literacy connections.

Children who cook take pride in what they make and are more likely to try new foods. A cooking program that emphasizes putting safety and health first also will enable children to cook in safety, become food literate, and to form healthy food patterns that will serve them well through out life.

Children also learn nutrition and eating habits in the home, which is a good reason for involving families in the cooking program in various ways, as discussed in the next chapter, WHAT'S COOKING WITH FAMILIES? And since lots of parents and grandparents like cooking, recruiting their help with it yields practical benefits and enjoyment all around.

4

What's Cooking with Families?

Anyone who works with young children can attest to the power of partnering with families. Partnership can take many forms in any area of the early childhood program, and cooking is no exception. Families may choose to volunteer in the classroom, accompany children on food-related field trips, attend special program-related functions, support teachers by providing family recipes, attend cooking-related workshops, or promote cooking with their children at home. For most families, cooking with children is something they are comfortable doing because it's already a part of their daily lives.

Parents in the classroom

Having parents or other family members cook with children in the classroom is also one of the best ways to make sure that your program represents the diversity of the children's families. Ask for recipe suggestions. Start with family favorites. Emphasize that you would particularly like recipes that reflect the family's heritage. Either working together with parents or on your own, you can turn these recipes into pictographic recipe cards that children can use in the cooking center (more information on making recipe cards can be found in the introduction to Part Two). You may need to make adaptations to the recipes either because they are too complicated or because certain ingredients are difficult to locate, too expensive, or unlikely to appeal to young children's palates.

Consider the following account of how a preschool teacher named Kay went about including 4-year-old Junior Selman's mother in a class cooking activity. During a home visit, Kay and Junior's mother, Ruth

Selman, discussed Junior's enthusiasm for dramatization. As an example, Kay described for Mrs. Selman how Junior loved to make and serve pretend callaloo soup to his classmates when in the housekeeping area. In response to Kay's request for more information about callaloo soup, Ruth told Kay that it was a typical dish from her native Trinidad. "Think spicy spinach soup, and you'll have an idea what callaloo soup tastes like." Kay then took the opportunity to ask Ruth whether she might be willing to help the children make callaloo soup in class.

Although taken with the idea, Mrs. Selman expressed concern about being able to supervise a whole class of 4-year-old cooks. Kay confidently assured her that no more than six children would be cooking at a time and that either she or her assistant teacher, Dana, would be on hand to help. Working together, Mrs. Selman dictated the following recipe for callaloo soup to Kay:

Ingredients:
1 lb. callaloo leaves
6 cups chicken stock
1 onion, finely chopped
1 clove garlic, chopped
2–3 scallions, chopped
¼ tsp. thyme
4 oz. lean salt pork, cut in small cubes
½ lb. crabmeat
½ cup fresh coconut milk
½ lb. okra
salt and pepper
several drops of Tabasco sauce

Directions: Wash greens and chop coarsely. Put in heavy saucepan with chicken stock, onion, garlic, scallions, thyme, and salt pork. Cover and cook at a simmer until the salt pork is tender. Crack coconut, and drain mik. Add crabmeat, coconut milk, and okra and cook until okra is done, about 10 minutes. Season to taste with salt, pepper, and Tabasco. Serves 6.

With recipe in hand, Kay and Ruth took a critical look at it, noting ingredients that might be difficult to find, expensive to purchase, hard for young cooks to manipulate, or likely to taste too strong. The table opposite shows the problems they analyzed and the solutions they came up with. With these changes, Ruth and Kay made the following recipe cards for the children to use:

Card #1: Wash spinach.
Card #2: Tear spinach into small pieces.
Card #3: Chop onion, garlic, scallions, and thyme.
Card #4: Chop ham into chunks.

Challenges Related to Making Callaloo Soup	
Problem	*Solution*
Callaloo isn't readily available.	Mrs. Selman confirmed that callaloo leaves come from the dasheen bush that grows only in tropical places. She suggested using spinach, bok choy, or Swiss chard as a substitute. They decided on using spinach because it was readily available at nearby grocery stores.
Homemade chicken stock requires too much preparation for 4-year-olds.	They decided to use canned chicken broth or chicken bouillon cubes.
Salt pork is not a healthy choice.	They felt that ham was a healthier food choice.
Crabmeat is expensive. Also, Samanda (one of Junior's classmates) is allergic to shellfish.	At Ruth's suggestion, they dropped crabmeat from the recipe.
Cracking open a coconut requires using tools that are not safe for preschoolers.	They decided that either Mrs. Selman will demonstrate for the children how to crack open a coconut or they will substitute a can of unsweetened coconut milk.
Fresh okra is not available this time of year.	They opted to use frozen okra. Consulting a cookbook, they found that a 10-oz. package of frozen okra is equivalent to ½ pound of fresh okra.
Tabasco sauce is likely too spicy for most of the children.	They decided to eliminate it from the recipe, offering children the option of a milder sauce such as Pickapeppa.

Card #5: Put everything in saucepan. Add chicken broth.
Card #6: Cover. Let simmer for 10 minutes.
Card #7: Add coconut milk and okra. Cook for 10 minutes.
Card #8: Add salt and pepper. Stir.
Card #9: Ladle into bowls. Serve.
Card #10: "Thank you, Mrs. Selman!"

Several days before Mrs. Selman was scheduled to cook with the children, Kay went over the recipe cards with her to make sure they were both comfortable with what had to be done. On the Wednesday morning that Mrs. Selman was coming to her class, Kay made sure that all of the necessary equipment was on hand: a chef's knife and cutting board, saucepan and lid, can opener, wooden spoon, timer, ladle, and soup bowls with soupspoons.

At the morning meeting, Kay announced to the children that, as a special treat, Junior's mother was going to be working with them in the cooking area to make one of Junior's and his family's favorites, callaloo soup. She reminded them that only six children could be in the cooking area with Mrs. Selman at one time. However, if others wanted a turn, Mrs. Selman promised to help them to make another batch or two.

As the children cooked with Mrs. Selman, Kay led them in observing the process and talking about what was happening. She asked them,

- "Who would like to try a piece of raw spinach? Does it taste like any other vegetables you've had?"
- "How do leafy green vegetables like spinach help our bodies grow?"
- "Who remembers what we can do to make our eyes not hurt when cutting onions?"
- "What can we do to get the smell of garlic off our fingers?"
- "How can we get the thyme leaves off the stems?"
- "In what ways are the scallions like the big onions? How are they different?"
- "What do you think will happen to the spinach when we cook it?"
- "What does stirring in the coconut milk do?"
- "Why do you think this is called a soup?"
- "How will we know when the soup is done? What do you think would happen to the soup if we kept cooking it after it's done?"
- "How many ladles of soup do you think it will take to fill a bowl?"
- "Who can tell us what the callaloo soup tastes like?"
- "What was your favorite part about making the soup?"

In addition to interacting with the children while they were cooking with Mrs. Selman, Kay took photos to document the experience. Later, Kay hung the photos on the bulletin board with captions. She also placed some of the photos in the children's portfolios to illustrate how they were learning skills such as measurement and hand-eye coordination through the cooking activity.

Later in the week, Kay followed up the cooking experience by talking with the children about the word *callaloo*. She explained that, to West Indians, callaloo is not just the name of a particular vegetable or a soup— it also means any mixture of great variety. Anything that is all mixed together is said to be a callaloo.

To further the children's knowledge about Trinidad, Kay read aloud the storybook *Baby-O*, by Nancy White Carlstrom. In that story, a West Indian family's song describes daily life to the beat of varying tempos.

Chickens running in the garden patch,
Running in the morning sun.
Try and catch.
Chuka Chuka,
Chuka Chuka.

Because the children kept mentioning Trinidad in their conversations with one another and with Kay, she decided it was a good topic for further study. Through their investigations at the library and on the Internet, the children discovered that Trinidad was the birthplace of the steel drum and calypso music. Trinidad's famous Carnival, they found out, could be described as a callaloo of people, costumes, music, and dancing. Kay invited Mrs. Selman back to tell the children more about the country, its people, and its foods.

Through these experiences, the children learned about the food, the people, the music, and life in tropical Trinidad. Their learning occurred through natural investigations that flowed from the original experience of cooking with Mrs. Selman.

One last point should be made about Kay's efforts to introduce diversity into her program. Though food and music were an entry point into the children's study of Trinidad, Kay avoided treating the subject in a "tourist curriculum" manner. By encouraging and supporting the children's investigations, she attempted to give children a deeper glimpse of the island's culture and daily life, building on the children's own questions. The preschoolers in Kay's class now have a good basic understanding of Junior's and his family's West Indian culture.

Let's go: Parents on field trips

Another way to bring families into cooking activities is to enlist family members to accompany the class on field trips that are related to cooking and food preparation. Think of family members not simply as extra adults for managing the children, but as sources of knowledge who can contribute to the value of a trip to a dairy, a farm, or an orchard.

Ms. Reynolds's class trip to a pick-your-own strawberry farm one sunny May morning illustrates how this can work. Five-year-old Pam's mom, Mrs. Gustafson, was one of three parents who went with the children and teachers to a nearby farm to pick strawberries. Mrs. Gustafson had mentioned that she grew strawberries in her own garden. At Ms.

Reynolds's suggestion, Mrs. Gustafson came to the class ahead of time to tell the children what to look for when they went berry picking. She told them to search for berries that were dry, firm, and very red. She also cautioned them against picking the largest berries, explaining that they were likely to be less tasty than smaller ones because they were probably filled with water from recent thunderstorms.

On the day that the class journeyed to the pick-your-own farm, Ms. Reynolds asked Mrs. Gustafson to first brief the other adult volunteers with information about strawberries and berry picking. The adults then reviewed with the children some tips for picking strawberries at the farm:

• Pull the berry from the stem with a slight twisting motion.

• Allow the berry to roll into the palm of your hand.

• Carefully place—don't throw—the fruit into your container.

• Don't overfill your container or try to pack the berries down.

At the farm, Mrs. Gustafson and the other parent volunteers each worked with just a few children in the field. They guided them through the exciting process of picking berries, filling the special berry baskets with plump, fresh strawberries, and occasionally tasting a berry to make sure the row was sweet!

Family evenings

A classroom cooking experience with families can be fun and provides opportunities for increasing parents' desire to cook with their children at home. At first, some parents may be hesitant to involve their young children in cooking. Fearing an accident or walls covered with spaghetti sauce, parents may be skeptical. However, once they see cooking's many benefits—and realize what young children are able to do—most parents welcome the idea of making their kitchen a safe and welcoming place for young chefs.

During a family evening, teachers can provide parents and other family members with concrete information on why cooking with children is important and how they can ensure that cooking experiences in their homes are positive for child and parent alike:

Give parents a sense of all the learning that goes on in cooking. For example, when children measure ingredients, they learn math; as they "read" recipe cards, they develop literacy skills; as they observe butter melt, they learn physical science; when muffin batter rises, they learn about volume; when they set the table with one place setting for each member of the family, they learn one-to-one correspondence. (The academic, cognitive, and social/emotional benefits of cooking are discussed in Chapter 5.)

Provide families with guidance on appropriate nutrition for young children. If parents are not already familiar with the USDA's Food Guide Pyramid for Young Children: A Daily Guide for 2- to 6-Year-Olds, introduce it to them. Better yet, provide each family with a poster of the Food Pyramid. Review with them the number of servings needed from each food group, and together share ideas for helping children reach those nutritional goals. For instance, ask "Does anyone have tips for parents whose children hate vegetables?" Together with family members, go through the process of analyzing the nutritional content of various foods.

Explain to families how you have childproofed the classroom cooking area to prevent accidents and illness. Share with them hints that they might use in their own homes. Family child care providers can give parents a tour of their kitchens so parents can observe firsthand how to cover outlets, what first-aid supplies to have on hand, and so forth.

Go over appropriate cooking techniques that parents might be interested in learning more about. For example, you can provide guidance on how children can safely use knives, grinders, graters, and the like.

Encouraging families to cook with their children

Teachers can involve families with cooking in various ways, but inspiring parents to include their children in home cooking activities will have the most lasting effect. Family evenings are one way to encourage parents, but other methods are also effective. Consider these ideas:

Whenever a child completes a recipe at school, send it home. Children will be thrilled to make the same recipes at home that they have cooked at school. Experience makes them experts, and they will love to tell their parents and siblings how the recipe should be done. If possible, gather the class recipes into a cookbook that can be presented to each family. In addition to the recipes, include recipe cards that parents can cut out or transfer to index cards. Photos and comments on the recipes will be especially welcome. You might even have children review the recipes and provide the names of children who picked each one as their favorite.

Let parents know, too, that they can include children in cooking activities even if they don't want their child to make an entire recipe. As parents make meals, children can assist in these efforts. Suggest that

parents assign their child specific tasks such as washing fruits and vegetables or draining pasta in a colander. Children can readily snap off the ends of green beans, peel the skins off fava beans, or mash a banana. Children also can help by making lists with their parent for grocery shopping, creating dinner or breakfast menus, or making placemats. In addition, parents can elicit their children's help in setting up a family recycling system or compost pile.

Encourage parents to use cooking experiences as conversational times. Research underscores the importance of adult-child conversations during mealtimes in building vocabulary and literacy skills (Snow 2000; Dickinson & Tabors 2001). Parents can use cooking times as opportunities to talk with children about their own experiences with cooking and to predict what will happen as they cook. Moreover, chatting together while cooking is also an excellent way to strengthen the parent-child bond. And as they cook with their parents, children become more competent and proud to be contributing members of their family.

Cooking with children is enhanced when teachers reach out to family members. Making cooking a family affair multiplies the enjoyment of all involved, expands children's learning, and makes everyone more creative.

5

Learning to Cook = Cooking to Learn

Today's early childhood teachers are increasingly under pressure to focus on instruction that addresses mandated learning objectives. All 50 states have published standards outlining learning goals for children in kindergarten and above, and more than 35 states have or are developing standards for children below kindergarten age (Kagan, Scott-Little, & Frelow 2003). National programs such as Head Start and professional associations in specific disciplines such as the National Council of Teachers of Mathematics (NCTM) have also developed their own sets of learning outcomes or standards (Head Start 2001; NCTM 2000).

The early childhood years are indeed an important time for children to build a strong foundation for reading, writing, math, science, social studies, technology, and the arts. But exploration, play, and hands-on experiences—the hallmarks of good early education—are also critical. Happily, cooking experiences fill the bill on both counts. Cooking activities are intrinsically appealing to children, as well as being rich in opportunities for learning. With a well-planned cooking program, teachers don't have to sacrifice developmentally appropriate practices to help children achieve important learning outcomes.

Clearly, learning opportunities abound in the cooking context. And from what we know about the way children learn, they are highly motivated when learning occurs in a natural context (Bredekamp & Copple 1997; Edwards, Gandini, & Forman 1998). Their experiences will inspire them to keep on cooking and keep on learning.

How cooking addresses learning goals

Nearly everything a child does while working on a recipe can lead to learning. Certainly young chefs learn about nutrition as they and their teacher discuss a recipe's relative health benefits. But children's learning also extends into traditional curriculum areas and learning domains.

Language and literacy

Much national attention has been focused on literacy. Early language and literacy goals include the following (NAEYC & IRA 1998):

• Oral language and vocabulary development

• Phonological awareness

• Knowledge of print and its uses

• Background knowledge to enable children to comprehend what they read

• Letter and word knowledge

In cooking with young children, teachers can address learning goals in a functional way. Children develop literacy skills when using short, structured samples of print such as recipe cards, charts, and menus and when reading books featuring cooking or food. (The box **Linking Cooking to Children's Experiences with Books and Music** on pages 54–55 offers some suggestions.) As they follow the pictures and accompanying written instructions on a recipe card, children learn that print goes from left to right and top to bottom and that the elements are read in a sequence. Sometimes children use the pictures on the cards to help them figure out what the recipe is saying. In trying to "read" recipe cards, children are quite motivated to decode what the print says.

Children also gain further knowledge of print as they consult shelf labels for stored cooking utensils such as colanders, whisks, and spatulas. As they see print on food packaging or create menus for their restaurant in the dramatic play area, they learn that print provides useful information.

Opportunities for teachers to introduce the alphabetic principle and letter-sound associations arise as children read through a recipe chart or card or as they work on writing one of their own. As teachers go over the cards with children, they can make comments or ask questions that focus children's attention on letters and sounds ("This recipe has lots of *p* words, doesn't it? Let's see just how many *p* words there are"). In the cooking area, children practice writing the letters in their names and associating those letters with the sounds in their names as they sign a sheet of paper indicating they've helped themselves to the snack (which also lets the teacher track whether all the children have remembered to snack that day).

Many opportunities for vocabulary development arise in learning to cook. Cooking has its own vocabulary—such as *baste, sauté,* and *knead*—and also introduces children to vocabulary that they will use in their everyday play and conversations, for example, *measure, combine, flavor,* and *spread*. Teachers can introduce words to children in a variety of ways. They may define ("*Blending* is mixing things together"), model ("See, this is *kneading*"), or infuse new words into their questions and comments ("This lemon tastes sour; it has a sour *flavor*").

Teachers can begin to instruct children in phonological awareness, too, by sharing food-related songs and rhymes with children (again, see **Linking Cooking to Children's Experiences with Books and Music**). Adults can also involve children in playing with the natural sounds of cooking, as the following teacher does.

> The children watch a frying egg, fascinated. "When an egg is cooking in a frying pan, it's sizzling. What does sizzling sound like?" asks Mrs. Bloom. "Sssssssssssssss!" hisses Charlie. "No, it's more crackly," says Maria. "Like crackitycricklecrack!"

Noticing sounds and trying to reproduce them enhances children's awareness of the sounds of language, which is key in learning to read and write.

Mathematics

Cooking and math go hand in hand. Measuring, learning about quantity and volume, exploring numbers, and learning the geometric concepts of shape, size, position, and direction are all integral parts of cooking. Teachers can use the many opportunities in cooking to introduce and reinforce mathematical processes and concepts. Many state math standards for preschool and kindergarten are based on NCTM's *Principles and Standards for School Mathematics* (NCTM 2000). The NCTM standards are divided into two groups: (1) mathematical *processes* that children need to acquire to do mathematics and (2) mathematical *content* that children should know.

To become mathematical thinkers, children need to learn process skills that involve solving problems, reasoning, making connections, communicating mathematically, and using and interpreting representations. Early childhood educators can teach children math process skills in authentic ways through cooking. For example, when a teacher asks a

Linking Cooking to Children's Experiences with Books and Music

Books on food and cooking-related subjects can be used to enhance children's learning and to help them make connections among different curriculum areas. The home or classroom library is a natural setting for introducing children to cooking-related picture books. Educators can begin by reading books aloud and discussing their food-related messages.

See the RESOURCES section for an extended list of recommended titles. The following list is just a sampling:

- *Blueberries for Sal*
- *Blue Moon Soup: A Family Cookbook*
- *Bon Appetit, Bertie!*
- *Bread and Jam for Frances*
- *Chicken Soup with Rice*
- *Dinner at the Panda Palace*
- *Dinner from Dirt*
- *Frog Goes to Dinner*
- *Frank and Ernest*
- *Pancakes for Breakfast*
- *Possum Magic*
- *Rain Makes Applesauce*
- *Sheep Out to Eat*

To make these books come alive, follow up by having the children cook some of the foods they've just read about. A few of the recipes in Part Two will help children bring to life the foods that the authors have written about, such as the recipes *Dr. Seuss' Green Eggs and Ham* (on p. 78) and *Stone Soup (Like in the Book)* (on p. 117).

There also are whole books devoted to enhancing children's joint enjoyment of literature and cooking. Some recommended titles include *Storybook Stew* (Barchers & Rauen 1997), *Holiday Storybook Stew* (Barchers & Rauen 1998), and *Cooking Up a Story* (Catron & Parks 1987).

Check out programs such as "Books on the Menu" from Reading Is Fundamental (RIF), which uses food-related books as the basis for cross-age literacy activities. The RIF program encourages the oldest students in an elementary school to mentor kindergartners in reading: "Through this food-themed initiative, children satisfy their craving for good books and stories while building new friendships." (For more information, visit www.rif.org/what/menu/default.mspx.)

Children will also enjoy food-related songs and rhymes. For example, an ideal introduction to the recipe *Pancake Puff* (p. 101) or *You Take the Pancake* (p. 79) is the following rhyme by poet Christina Rossetti.

> Mixin' pancakes
> Stirrin' pancakes
> Pop 'em in the pan
> Fryin' pancakes
> Flippin' pancakes
> Catch 'em if you can!

Songs about food that can be used as a lead-in or follow-up to cooking include the following.

These albums, cassettes, and CDs contain selections of food-related songs:

- *Angel Food Cake* (Cynthia Todd)—contact Alpenhorn Press at alpentodd@yahoo.com
- *Beans for Brunch* (Jory Aronson)—www.jorysings.com
- *Bon Appetit! Musical Food Fun* (Cathy Fink and Marcy Marxer)—www.bonappetit.cathymarcy.com
- *Fruit Salad* (Jory Aronson)—www.jorysings.com
- *Fun Food Songs* (Tom Paxton)—www.amazon.com
- *Garden Party* (Cynthia Todd)—contact Alpenhorn Press at alpentodd@yahoo.com
- *What Goes with Peanut Butter* (Jory Aronson)—www.jorysings.com

Some albums offer a food-related song or two among others on other subjects:

- "Annie, My Cooking Friend" on *Jambo and Other Call & Response Songs and Chants* (Ella Jenkins)—www.folkways.si.edu
- "The Fruit Song" on *The Big Picture & Other Songs for Kids* (The Chenille Sisters)—www.cantoorecords.com
- "I Am a Pizza" on *Wha'D'Ya Wanna Do?* (Peter Alsop)—www.peteralsop.com
- "Peanut Butter Sandwich" on *Singable Songs for the Very Young: Great with a Peanut-Butter Sandwich* (Raffi)—www.amazon.com

- "The VegaBoogie" on *Circle Around: Celebrating Life Through Music and Dance* (Tickle Toon Typhoon)—http://tickletunetyphoon.com

These fun songs, not necessarily written for children but still food-focused, are available as downloads:

- "Bangers and Mash" (Peter Sellers)—www.mp3.com
- "Bread and Butter" (The Newbeats)—www.mp3.com
- "On Top of Spaghetti" (Tom Glazer)—www.wtv-zone.com/REMEMBERTHEN/lyrics/musiclyricsy.html

Finally, here are some websites for children's songs and music:

- **www.kididdles.com**—Lyrics of children's songs (some with audio) by subject. Includes song search bulletin board. Food songs include:

    "Apples and Bananas"
    "The Muffin Man"
    "Pancakes"
    "Peanut Butter and Jelly"
    "Popcorn!"
    "Raisins and Almonds"
    "Short'nin' Bread"

- **www.kidsmusicweb.com**—Quick guide to kids music resources on the Web.
- **www.childrensmusic.org**—A nonprofit resource for children, families, and children's performers worldwide.
- **www.cdbaby.com**—A comprehensive list of children's artists' websites, including ordering information and reviews.

child who is working with dough how she can divide the dough into two pieces that are the same size, the teacher encourages the child to think about the problem and come up with a strategy that makes sense to her. The problem has more than one right answer, so the child must reflect on the task and test out hypotheses that she thinks might work. For example, the child might try eyeballing the dough and tearing it into two pieces, which she then lines up next to each other for comparison. If one piece is larger, she can make adjustments by taking some dough from the larger piece and adding it to the smaller piece. Alternatively, she may decide to use a balance to weigh the pieces until they are equal or a ruler to measure their length.

To refine children's reasoning skills, teachers can focus children's attention on categories, focusing on one or two attributes at a time: "Dougie, could you please get all the large [size], white [color] mixing bowls and bring them over to the table so we can start our recipe?" Copley suggests that teachers ask questions such as the following to foster children's math reasoning skills:

- Are you sure?
- How do you know?
- Why do you think . . . ?
- What else can you find that works like this?
- What would happen if . . . ?
- I wonder how this could be changed?
- What would the pattern be?
- What if . . . ?
- I wonder why . . . ?
- Perhaps it's because . . . ? (2000, 37)

Helping children make connections between math and cooking experiences is an ongoing process. The teacher's role is to help children relate the intuitive mathematical principles they have discovered on their own to the more formal principles of math. Questions and comments such as the following engage children in using mathematical processes to approach real problems:

- "Could you please set a fork at each chair, so everyone in our group can eat the fruit salad we made?"
- "Can you guess (or estimate) how many bananas we'll need to make a smoothie?"
- "How can we cut these sandwiches to get two triangles?"
- "I wonder how many cups of water this pitcher will hold?"

- "What setting should we use on the timer so it beeps after 3 minutes to tell us the soft-boiled eggs are done?"
- "Elizabeth is 5 today. Can you get out the candles we'll need to put on her birthday cake?"

Children also need specific content knowledge to think mathematically. Again, teachers can highlight and reinforce these knowledge concepts in cooking activities. For example, nearly every recipe involves the concepts of number and quantity. To add 2 teaspoons of vanilla or work out how to fit 12 scoops of batter on the cookie sheet, for example, children encounter numbers and quantities in a situation where these concepts really matter. Or as they try to set the table with the same number of napkins as there are chairs, children are engaged in trying to create one-to-one correspondence.

Concepts of geometry and spatial sense come into play during cooking activities as children fill a mold with tuna salad, decide how to fit all the slices of bread on the toaster oven rack, or use shaped cookie cutters to cut cheese slices or tea sandwiches. Children encounter patterning ideas when they weave strips of piecrust into a latticework top crust, layer a composed salad, or make lasagna. Similarly, to duplicate the arrangement of a fruit and cheese platter they see in a cookbook photo, children must work to recognize and replicate the pattern (e.g., two strips of cheese after every pear slice).

Teachers can get children working with measurement concepts by challenging them to figure out how many cups are in a quart or how many teaspoons in a tablespoon. The following example explores this concept in action:

> While making *Bag o' (Whole Wheat) Bread*, Jordie is stumped as to how to add 1½ cups of flour to the mixing bag. His teacher, Miss Curry, encourages him to look over the measuring cups and study the numbers on them. Jordie, with help from the group, recognizes that he'll need both the 1-cup and the ½-cup measures. Using a scoop, he fills both measuring cups with flour. Then, as Miss Curry had demonstrated earlier, he lifts each cup, one at a time, over a bowl and draws the edge of a metal spatula across its top, allowing the excess flour to fall into the bowl. With great fanfare, he carefully empties the 1-cup and ½-cup measures of flour into the mixing bag, as Miss Curry lets out a triumphant "Ta-da!"

In the book *The Power of Projects* (Helm & Beneke 2003), teacher Marilyn Worsley relates how a project on pizza with a multiage classroom of children ages 3–5 enabled her to teach mathematics to the benchmarks

Ways That a Pizza Project Relates to Math Learning Standards

Math Standard	Activities from the Pizza Project
Explore concepts such as quantity, number, counting, and one-to-one correspondence	• Played numeral match games (matched numeral to slices of pizza with varying number of pepperoni) • Followed simple recipes to cook pizza • Made tally marks on field drawings to record the quantity of buckets, cans, and wheels seen at the restaurant • Used tape measure in constructing models of items such as pizza warmer and cheese/sausage grinder • Decided how many pizzas to order for family pizza party
Connect number words to quantities they represent using physical models and representations	• Voted for project topic and recorded votes on voting chart • Used measuring tape to construct pizza warmer and cheese/sausage grinder • Decided how many pizzas to order for family pizza party • Played numeral match games (matched numeral to slices of pizza with varying number of pepperoni) • Used a recipe to determine quantities to be measured and added to make pizza dough and sauce
Solve simple mathematical problems	• Decided how long pieces of cardboard and paper should be when constructing models of a pizza warmer and cheese grinder • Decided how many pizzas to order for family pizza party
Make comparisons of quantities and show understanding of and use of comparative words	• Grated piles of paraffin at the water table and compared sizes of piles • Discussed voting chart and decided which project topic had more votes • Discussed how tall and wide the model pizza warmer and sausage/cheese grinder should be

Math Standard	Activities from the Pizza Project
	• Built a pizza warmer and sausage/cheese grinder using predetermined measurements • Tallied the types of pizza for family pizza night
Use tools to measure	• Measured to construct pizza warmer and sausage/cheese grinder using yardstick and tape measure
Sort and classify objects by a variety of properties	• Played a vegetable "feely game" in which the children guess what they are touching • Played with flannelboard pizza and flannel ingredients • Guessed pizza ingredients based on their smell
Describe qualitative change	• Experimented with yeast and the way it causes dough to rise • Observed that rotting tomatoes became flatter • Noted changes in pizza ingredients when baked (cheese melted and bubbled, crust turned brown)
Represent data using concrete objects, pictures, and graphs	• Voted for topic and recorded votes on voting chart • Tallied wheels and containers in field sketches • Sketched what was seen on field-site visit • Drew pizza tools • Sculpted clay models of pizza tools • Drafted construction plans for model pizza warmer and sausage/cheese grinder • Graphed type of pizza each family eats and likely number of slices per family member

Adapted by permission from J.H. Helm, S. Beneke, & M. Worsley, "Meeting Standards Effectively, " in *The Power of Projects: Meeting Contemporary Challenges in Early Childhood Classrooms—Strategies and Solutions*, eds. J.H. Helm & S. Beneke, (New York: Teachers College Press; Washington, DC: NAEYC, 2003), 93–95. Copyright © 2003 by Teachers College Press, Columbia University. All rights reserved.

of the Illinois Early Learning Standards. During their in-depth, long-term study, children studied and explored pizza through a variety of means—class discussions, reading books about pizza, field trips to a pizza parlor, and more—culminating in a family pizza party. The table **Ways That a Pizza Project Relates to Math Learning Standards** on pages 58–59 shows just some of the aspects of the pizza project that Worsley identifies as related to math processes and, in particular, to the Illinois standards. Some of the activities are noted as relating to more than one standard. The project also integrated other curriculum areas in addition to math, including language arts and science.

Clearly, cooking can be a powerful tool for meeting the kinds of goals identified as important for math in the early years. In cooking, children learn the processes and content of math through their interactions with materials and problem situations as well as through thoughtful teacher questions and comments.

Science

For young children, science is about making sense of the world around them. Children acquire the fundamental concepts of science through active exploration, interactions with their environment, and adults who share information and ideas with them. For example, science education may occur when Juwan asks why popcorn kernels pop in a microwave oven or when Amy wonders what causes bread dough to rise. As these children cook and observe the changes in physical properties and chemical reactions, they are able to learn about science—not in the theoretical sense, but in action. Their knowledge is not complete, of course; but they can acquire many concepts that science educators see as foundational. They can also learn the process skills of scientific inquiry, including asking scientific questions, planning and conducting investigations, gathering data, and communicating findings.

Science-related process skills can be introduced through cooking in the

same authentic ways as math process skills are introduced. Indeed, math and science learning often take place together when young children cook. The scientific process calls for children to observe, predict, and test out theories—processes integral to both mathematics and science.

Teachers can model scientific questioning by wondering aloud:

- "What would happen if we added all the wet ingredients to the dry ingredients all at once, instead of a little bit at a time?"
- "How will we know when the muffins are ready to take out of the oven?"
- "What happens to the oobleck when you pick it up in your hands?"
- "Why do you think the cheese started to bubble in the toaster oven?"
- "How would you describe gak to someone who's never made it before?"

To encourage children to pose their own questions or do some investigating, teachers can ask questions of various types:

- What surprised you when we did . . . ?
- What do you want to find out?
- I'm wondering what would happen if we added more . . . ? (After children investigate that question, she might ask them, What are *you* wondering about?)
- What do we need to know to make . . . ?

The investigations that result from such questions are a natural part of cooking, as we saw in the project work on pizzas. In response to those questions, the children can begin to generate possible answers and ideas, which will lead to various investigations. Teachers can guide children in their investigations by picking up on children's observations:

- "You're right, Tim, the dough didn't rise like it was supposed to. What do you think went wrong? We can experiment. Shall we try giving it more time?" (Then, depending on the results, the teacher might suggest trying one portion of the dough in a warmer place and another in a cooler place, and so on.).
- "You think our ice cream turned out too soupy? I think you're right. If we want the ice cream to be firmer, what could we try?" (If the children need further prompting, the teacher might suggest trying more or less ice or salt.)

To pursue their investigations and answer their questions, children can learn to gather data by being good observers. Teachers can further this process by heightening children's sensory awareness:

- "What does dry yeast look like?"
- "How would you describe the skin of a kiwi?"
- "How does the sound of popcorn popping change the longer it's in the microwave?"
- "What does this fennel smell like to you?"
- "Taste a piece of pickled ginger and tell us what it's like."

The most obvious and direct product of children's investigations and labors is the food they prepare. For example, after testing how much salt and ice must be added to the outer bag to adequately freeze the ingredients in *Ice Cream in a Bag* (see p. 95) the most popular way to "communicate findings" is to treat everyone to the final product! Of course, other ways can be used to represent collected data. Teachers can show children how to make graphs depicting which recipes were the most popular. Children might want to draw or paint a completed recipe, tape-record spoken versions of the recipe and directions, or take photographs (or arrange the photos a teacher takes) to document the steps they followed and the results they got.

Recipes can be a starting point for some interesting scientific explorations. For example, after children make the snack recipe *Queen Bean Dip* (p. 111) or another recipe made with seeds or beans, teachers can explain that foods such as beans start out as tiny sprouts. Early childhood science expert Karen Lind notes that in growing foods such as mung beans, alfalfa sprouts, or lima beans as a class project, children encounter a number of principles and process skills relevant to science and math:

> [F]or a science investigation, kindergartners might be interested in the process of plant growth. Supplied with lima bean seeds, wet paper towels, and glass jars, the children place the seeds in the jars, securing the seeds to the sides of the jars with the paper towels. Each day they add water, if needed, and observe what is happening to the seeds. They dictate their observation to their teacher, who records their comments on a chart. Each child also plants some beans in dirt in a small container such as a paper or plastic cup. The teacher supplies each child with a chart for his or her bean garden. The children check off each day on their charts until they see a sprout. Then they count how many days it took for a sprout to appear, comparing this number with those of other class members, as well as with the time it takes for the seeds in the glass jars to sprout. The children have used the concepts of number and counting, one-to-one correspondence, time, and comparison of the number of items in two groups. (1999, 75–76)

In addition to learning scientific process skills, children of preschool and kindergarten age can begin learning the content areas of science: physical science, life science, earth science, and environmental science. Physical science is at the core of cooking activities. When children observe

cheese melting and ice cream freezing, they experience changes in the physical states of foods. They learn that heat can melt solids and that cold can freeze liquids. Observing the reversal of a transformation—for example, freezing and then melting a substance, or vice versa—introduces children to a fundamental aspect of physical science. Children learn about the physical properties of foods up close, through hands-on activities. For example, when testing for the freshness of eggs, children see how the density of fresh versus spoiled eggs differs: Placed in a bowl of salty water, a fresh egg will sink whereas a spoiled egg will float to the top. Most children will enjoy ensuring that the eggs they are using in a recipe are fresh, using this "sink or float" test.

Experiences with food also enable young children to learn about life science. Teachers can talk with children and share books about where the ingredients they use in recipes come from. Corn is part of a tall plant; apples are produced on trees; potatoes grow underground; milk comes from cows, and so on. Children can also gain knowledge of the earth and the environment by growing plants for themselves. They can plant seeds in a dirt-filled paper cup, as described earlier, or suspend an avocado pit or a sweet potato eye with toothpicks in a jar of water. Later, these sprouts can be planted outside in a vegetable garden as a reminder that some plants not only are beautiful to look at but are often food sources too. Growing foods for use in cooking activities enables children of all ages to see life science in action.

Social studies

Social studies is the study of people and their surroundings. Multidisciplinary and interdisciplinary, social studies connects with every area of the curriculum. At the early childhood level, social studies significantly overlaps with promoting children's socioemotional development, which is discussed later in this chapter. This is because learning social studies skills in the early years starts with the children themselves and the groups they live in: families, classrooms, and communities. And, as with math and science, social studies involves both process outcomes and content outcomes that children should achieve.

The process skills of social studies focus on investigation. They include identifying problems, gathering information, analyzing information, and drawing conclusions. Each of these four process skills can be taught and reinforced through cooking. Teachers can pose questions and suggestions such as the following to help children identify a problem and target ideas for study:

- "We've got a lot of different types of trash here. Where should we put them? Can we recycle any of our trash?"
- "Do you think someone who is a vegetarian would eat baloney roll-ups?"
- "Not everyone eats the same kind of food. Let's look at the recipes in our class cookbook and talk about the ones that our families often eat."

To encourage children to gather information about cooking activities, a teacher might bring in related books or suggest that children use the Internet (in the classroom or at home) with an adult to find out more. For example, when learning about Korean foods or making a Korean recipe, children can do some research to find out about traditional Korean culture and its cooking and eating styles. Then when Mrs. Han comes to the class to make kim chi with the children, they will have questions and comments for her.

Projects in the social studies domain often delve into cooking-related areas. For example, children might look at the commonalities of foods across cultures. In addition to books that explore this topic (for example, *Everybody Bakes Bread* and *Everybody Cooks Rice*, both by Norah Dooley, children can research the dough-covered foods that almost every country delights in. For example, there are samosas from India, pierogies from Poland, empañadas from Mexico, spanakopita from Greece, calzones from Italy, spring rolls from Vietnam, and pigs-in-a-blanket from the United States.

The content of social studies in preschool and kindergarten includes geographical (spatial) thinking, people and how they live, people and the environment, and people and the past. In the early learning years, the geography part of the curriculum often centers on the physical spaces that children know best and those that they encounter. Early mapping skills draw on and develop children's spatial understanding as well as lay the groundwork for map use in geography. They can be developed as children locate a certain part of the grocery store, orchard, or other food-related site from a simple map. Or children can help to design the layout for the eating and work spaces in the classroom, representing these in a map.

Young children can learn about people and how they live by looking to their own families. Children may discuss how meals are eaten at their homes, as well as who is responsible for setting the table and who for cleaning up. Teachers can then relate this information to how children eat snacks and meals in their classroom and what each person's role is in making these activities work well. In field trips to community markets and grocery stores, or possibly a farm or dairy, children could interview the people who work there to find out about their jobs and how they contribute to supplying the foods that the children use in their recipes.

Even young children can become more aware of the environment and begin to understand the importance of managing our natural resources. Teachers could invite facility managers, scientists, and environmental advocates to the classroom or talk to rangers, engineers, and other experts on field trips to parks, landfills, and other sites. These experts can explain and demonstrate to children the challenges of protecting our air, water, soil, and other parts of nature while providing the energy, water, and other materials humans need. And they, along with teachers, can help children see the connection between care of our environment and the food we eat. Children can learn to care for the classroom environment through minimizing waste (by reusing paper or homemade playdough, for example), making compost for a class garden, and similar conservation activities. Teachers and children can discuss the local community's recycling guidelines, and children can separate the trash they generate from cooking and other activities into containers for the paper, plastic, glass, and metal. Teachers are often surprised at how interested children are in environment-friendly practices.

Cooking favorite family recipes is a good way to involve children in learning about different family traditions and histories. Teachers can solicit family support in this effort by, for example, having parents and extended family members contribute treasured family recipes for a class cookbook. Family members might participate in making recipe cards for the recipes they've supplied, or even lead small groups in making the recipes. One enjoyable event might be to present all of the dishes the children have made from the family favorites at a potluck open house. Parents and grandparents can also tell and show children how cooking and some recipes have changed over time with technology (e.g., cooking popcorn on the stove in a pot with oil versus in the microwave). For more about family involvement in cooking see Chapter 4, WHAT'S COOKING WITH FAMILIES?

The arts

Although all of the arts can be linked with food and cooking activities, the visual arts relate most naturally to classroom cooking. We all know from experience that the more appealing foods look, the more likely we are to enjoy cooking and eating them. Viewing photos in cookbooks

and leafing through the colorful drawings in picture books such as Marcia Vaughan's *Tingo Tango Mango Tree* can play a role in inspiring young readers to cook themselves. The RESOURCES section provides a listing of children's picture books with food-related themes. Any of these books can be read and shared with children and used as an entry into related cooking activities. *Green Eggs and Ham* and *Stone Soup* may be the best known picture books with a cooking theme, but libraries have dozens of titles that teachers can use to relate to cooking activities. *Green Eggs and Ham* may also motivate children to explore how color affects our reactions to food (e.g., "Why would green eggs—or blue cake—likely not appeal to many people?").

Many great artists have created works depicting foods, and children can begin to enjoy these. One of Cezanne's still life paintings of fruit, such as the one on this page, can stir both children's artistic sense and their interest in cooking and making visually appealing creations. Children define their own aesthetic sense as they experiment with arranging finished dishes on a plate, creating patterns, and reproducing creations from the images in books and museum fine art reproductions. Children can experiment with color, pattern, and design as they craft artistic displays of their culinary creations.

In the art area, children can make their own restaurant and food props (such as models of different foods they've eaten or recipes they've made) to be used in their dramatic play. They might design menus, placemats, or other items. The class cookbook project previously described is one way to involve children in illustrating their interpretations of what the foods to be prepared will look like.

Familiarity with the properties of various art media can also be gained through cooking experiences. When children make any of the recipes for paint, chalk, or clay in ART AND SCIENCE RECIPES, they are actually creating art materials. Homemade art materials not only give children a sense of accomplishment in producing their own media but also allow children to play a creative role in choosing and manipulating colors, color intensity, texture or thickness, and other aspects of the medium.

Using these homemade media, children can then draw, paint, print, and sculpt their own interpretations of the dishes they make in cooking activities. For example, after making a dish like *Prizeworthy Pretzels* (p. 115), the bakers who shaped and braided the actual dough can now invent new (inedible) versions of the pretzels using clay.

Technology

Technology has a variety of connections with cooking experiences and learning. Teachers can help children use the Internet to search for particular recipes; to identify foods linked to specific climates, countries, and cultures; or to find out how foods such as milk and strawberries get from the farm to the classroom. In addition, children and adults can use word processing programs to store recipes or write a class cookbook and illustrate it with scanned-in student artwork.

Educators can also use computer programs to document their observations of children and demonstrate children's progress toward achieving learning outcomes. Taking digital photos helps to record and document the process of cooking. These images can then be downloaded and shown to parents as a slide show or printed out for display either on a bulletin board or within the cooking center. Data can be transferred to children's portfolios, shared at parent conferences, and used to track class progress. Computer-based technology has a use in countless ways by both children and educators to support cooking learning.

Beyond computer-based programs, mechanical tools and equipment are also often used in cooking. For instance, when children observe the way microwave ovens, stoves, and refrigerators work, they learn how these appliances change the physical properties of food. And as they explore and use gadgets such as eggbeaters, graters, corers, hullers, zesters, grinders, peelers, and egg slicers, children acquire fundamental understandings about tools, such as how they enable us to do things better or more easily. The children are challenged to think about the role of tools and technology in cooking: "How could we melt butter if we didn't have a microwave oven?" or "What's the difference between a whisk and an eggbeater?" Children who cook develop a better understanding of kitchen technology and can ultimately become proficient at using kitchen utensils and tools in safe and creative ways.

Fine-motor skill and development

Nearly every cooking action involves using the small muscles in the hand as well as refining hand-eye coordination. Whether using a knife to cut celery, a peeler to scrape carrots, a huller to clean strawberries, a colander to drain noodles, or an eggbeater to beat eggs, children are constantly refining their fine-motor skills. Teachers will, of course, need to guide young children in the safe use of cooking implements (see Chapter 3, PUTTING SAFETY AND HEALTH FIRST).

Most important, as they cook, children are developing these skills in a natural way. When teachers involve children in cooking activities and show them how to manipulate cooking tools, children will be much more likely to pick up a pizza cutter or a melon baller and use it as part of a cooking activity on their own. As they knead, stir, spread, and cut, children develop the hand strength and coordination they will also put to use in writing, drawing, and various life skills.

Socioemotional development

As noted earlier in this chapter, socioemotional development relates to the social studies curriculum, with an emphasis on both valuing others and learning to be socially competent. But socioemotional development also includes feeling safe and secure at school or family child care, learning to value one's self, being able to self-regulate, and exhibiting initiative. Socioemotional development, an important precursor to academic success (Shonkoff & Phillips 2000), is not something children can achieve entirely on their own; caring adults must form deep relationships with children and provide a warm classroom environment. Frequent, sensitive interactions in which adults let children know they are respected and valued lay the groundwork for strong bonds.

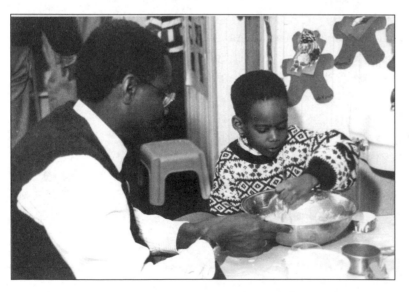

Of course, these interactions must take place throughout the day, in every area of the classroom. But during cooking activities, adults can interact with children in the following ways to support independence, persistence, and other aspects of socioemotional development:

- Allow children to choose when they want to be in the cooking area and which recipe to cook. In some cases, you may want to give them a few choices of what to make.
- Let children know that they can independently use much of the cooking equipment.
- Discuss with children what they like to eat and what they don't like.
- Help children to see tasks through to completion.
- Allow children to be creative in their cooking, which can mean allowing a child to alter a recipe to try out an idea or a preference.

Children feel competent when they make good choices and feel that their opinions are seriously considered. A positive self-concept also develops when children experience success and receive meaningful feedback. Commenting on children's specific skills alerts them to their progress. For example, telling Matthew that his skill in cutting has improved dramatically since the beginning of the year is more meaningful than the blanket comment "Good job!"

When teachers first introduce cooking tools in a controlled situation, they give children a chance to practice before using the equipment in a cooking activity. This practice period sets the stage for a successful cooking experience. Likewise, offering children a choice of two or three recipes —simple, and a bit more complex—will help determine successful cooking experiences. Letting children take personal responsibility for deciding what to eat, when to have their morning and afternoon snacks, and how much to eat (within reason) further supports children's sense of self.

Children's learning to self-regulate their behavior is a key goal for socioemotional development in the preschool years. Self-regulation enables children to balance their own wants with the rules of the classroom and the needs of other children. Such a balance is no easy feat at any age! Particularly for young children, two primary skills are involved: impulse control and delay of gratification. During cooking activities, teachers can encourage procedures that facilitate turn taking; for example, use of a timer or a sign-up sheet. Children soon learn that they have to wait but that they *will* get a turn. Setting limits and providing acceptable choices from which children can choose likewise contributes to children's developing ability to control impulses. Delayed gratification is inherently a component of the cooking process: Children don't have a dish to eat until they have completed the recipe they're working on. At lunchtime, children learn to wait to eat until all diners at a table have washed their hands and taken their seats.

Self-regulation also involves learning how to negotiate and to share—important life skills. The following scenario describes how two children solved a conflict over kitchen tools:

> Marcus was busy at the table in the cooking area making *Happy Trails Mix*. Jake, who was making another recipe at the table, went over to Marcus's area and took the 1-cup measure away. "Hey, I'm using that," Marcus yelled out. "Well, I need it, too," said Jake.
>
> Marcus then walked over to Jake's place and raised his arm, as if to grab back the measuring cup. He stopped himself, though, and instead asked Jake a question: "Do you need it for a long time or just a little bit?" "It will only be for one second," Jake let him know. "OK, you can use it then, Jake," Marcus responded. "But give it to me as soon as you're done. And if you want it next time, ask me. OK?" "OK," Jake agreed.

Children don't learn overnight the effective problem-solving skills that Marcus and Jake showed in this example. Teachers must continually model and discuss negotiation and sharing with children, offering positive feedback and constructive suggestions when appropriate.

Initiative—what Erikson (1950) described as the eagerness for more adventure and more responsibility—is another key aspect of young children's socioemotional development. One way to promote and support children's development of initiative is through room arrangement. The physical environment sends children messages about how welcome they are to play and learn in that space and to be responsible for themselves and, within limits, for their own choices. The cooking area is no exception. The table **Effects of Physical Arrangement on Children's Initiative** explores how the arrangement of the cooking area affects children's development. Erikson described the primary developmental task for children in the years from 3 to 6 as achieving a balance between taking initiative and learning to control their impulses.

Close observation and caring direction from their teachers during cooking activities can foster children's positive socioemotional development in all the areas discussed here.

Cognitive development and approaches to learning

Cognitive development refers to children's acquisition of thinking skills. In addition to subject-specific knowledge and skills, children need to develop fundamental cognitive abilities such as problem solving and planning. In addition, children's approaches to learning are vital to their success in school and in later life. These include children's curiosity, flexibility, initiative, and persistence.

It is perhaps in these approaches to learning that cooking is most valuable. As a subject area, cooking builds on children's natural motiva-

Effects of Physical Arrangement on Children's Initiative

Using this arrangement strategy . . .	Promotes initiative by . . .
Clearly organize cooking tools, with tool-shaped labels	Enabling children to get tools and equipment on their own and when finished to return tools to the appropriate place
Allow children at least 1 hour of choice time	Giving children enough time to see a cooking project through to completion
Make sure the cooking area includes walking space	Enabling children to maneuver in the area without fear of bumping into furniture or other cooks
Provide storage space	Allowing children to store a finished product that may not be eaten until later in the day
Provide duplicates of the most commonly used equipment and gadgets	Avoiding struggles over needed tools
Store electrical equipment and knives in locked cabinets out of children's reach, and let children use them only when supervised by an adult	Sending children the message that the cooking area is a safe place in which to work
Have safe-to-use cleaning supplies handy	Allowing children to clean up spills they have made and carry on with their efforts
Stock the area with real tools, in good condition	Reinforcing that children are cooking—not playing at cooking Valuing their work by providing real materials that make the task both appealing and safe

tion to cook. Besides fulfilling a basic need to eat, cooking affords children a rare opportunity to do something they see as very grown-up, an activity that adults do.

Children are curious to see how a recipe develops into something they can eat. Rare is the child who doesn't enjoy stirring batter in a bowl, observing the dry ingredients meld with the wet ingredients, and then delighting in the final edible product. As children pick recipes of their own choosing and as they are encouraged to make substitutions and add other ingredients, their creative juices flow. What if I added food coloring

to the batter? How can I make the muffins look fancier? What can I do to make it easier to eat the muffins without getting crumbs all over the place?

We know from motivation research that children who have choices in their activities and who can experience success are the most likely to become engaged and to persist in a task (Lumsden 1994). Both of these principles can be readily incorporated into cooking activities, as noted earlier. Sometimes by giving children a choice of two or three recipes in the cooking area, teachers can build in choice. Having something good to eat at the end of the activity is an additional motivation for learning to cook, following a recipe, and sticking with it through all the steps.

Children encounter many situations in which they are called on to use reasoning and problem solving. The pudding didn't thicken, so what should we do now? We want to separate the broth from the vegetables—what tool would allow us to do that? As adults lead children in cooking projects, it soon becomes clear that cooking can be a forum for experimenting, testing alternatives, and coming up with solutions. Children want their cooking projects to be successful. Learning to solve problems and capitalize on the solutions is part of what makes cooking so engrossing to the young chef.

Cooking is learning

As underscored in this chapter, cooking *is* learning. Cooking activities introduce children to the processes and subject matter content that preschoolers and kindergartners need to acquire, doing so in ways that make cooking an ideal vehicle for teaching and learning. Cooking may be unique in its ability to interweave learning goals and standards in an authentic, natural way. Learning becomes embedded in the cooking experience. Children who cook develop a healthy appetite, not only for food but also for learning.

PART TWO

Let's Get Cookin'!

Using Recipes with Young Children

At the heart of a successful cooking experience is the recipe. As adults, we use cookbooks to guide us. But how do we introduce nonreaders and beginning readers in preschool and kindergarten to recipes? The answer is through pictographic *recipe cards.*

Such recipe cards are like a rebus; through simple pictures and text, the card lets children know what needs to be done. Moreover, a recipe card breaks down a recipe into manageable steps. Children follow the cards in sequence until all of the tasks on the cards are completed.

The easiest way to explain what recipe cards look like is to show them. Here are the recipe cards for *Painted Toast* (on p. 77). As you can see, the cards

- show children how to make the entire recipe
- break down the task into discrete steps

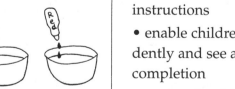
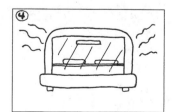

- provide picture and written clues so that beginning readers can follow the instructions
- enable children to work independently and see a task through to completion
- ensure the children have a successful cooking experience.

Most teachers put each recipe step on an individual index card (either 3x5 or 4x8) and laminate the cards. Including a title card for each recipe will help keep your sets of recipe cards organized. Laminating the cards allows easy cleanup and repeated use. The cards can be laid out on the cooking table or taped onto a wall in sequence. Some teachers like to make stands for their cards. For example, you can turn a paper cup upside down and cut a slit in the bottom to slide in a card. Another simple holder is a clothespin clipped to the bottom of a recipe card and then secured in a lump of clay or playdough.

Recipe chart

Some teachers use *recipe charts,* sometimes known as *cooking charts,* as a substitute for or supplement to recipe cards. The charts are identical to recipe cards, except that chart paper is used instead of file cards. Each step is drawn on a separate sheet of chart paper and then taped to a wall in sequence or placed on an easel to flip the pages as each step is completed. In much the same way that big books enhance the storybook reading experience, the larger chart paper is easier for some young children to follow than index cards. Still other teachers prefer to draw all of the cooking steps on one large sheet of chart paper and use a pointer to go through the steps in sequence. Some start by depicting all of the ingredients, much like a recipe in a cookbook begins by listing ingredients. They might introduce a recipe with charts and then, during the actual preparation process, offer index cards that the children can manipulate themselves.

Finding a Good Substitute

Making a recipe such as *Cheese-Louise Meatballs* (see p. 88) might be a good choice nutritionally for most children, as described in Chapter 3. But a child who is vegetarian or whose family keeps kosher, for example, could not participate in the activity. Many children have special dietary needs. Some are lactose intolerant or have other food allergies. In other cases, children may not eat certain foods for cultural or religious reasons, or because of family choice. Recipes can usually be adapted to fit individual needs.

Some of the recipes in this section list common variations to consider. But the number of possibilities is far too extensive and changing to address in this volume. Whatever the reason for substituting ingredients—personal preference, health reasons, or just running short of something—substitution lists abound in books available at your library and bookstore. There are also online resources to help cooks replace a recipe ingredient; here is just a sampling:

www.foodsubs.com

http://homecooking.about.com/od/substitutions1

www.foodallergy.org

http://asiarecipe.com/religion.html

And what about the *Meatballs* dilemma? To accommodate those children's needs and to make the recipe "dietary-friendly" for everyone, a teacher could use a grain-based meat substitute for the ground turkey the original recipe calls for.

To get a better idea of how recipe cards can be made to accompany any recipe, look at children's cookbooks on the market that make use of this technique. *Cup Cooking* (Foote 1999) and *Pretend Soup* (Katzen & Henderson 1994) are two of the better ones.

Here, in this book, all of the recipes readily lend themselves to the use of recipe cards and charts. In fact, each recipe was field tested with teachers who made their own recipe cards. With a little practice, you'll find that you too can make recipe cards with ease. With guidance, children themselves may sometimes help to make recipe cards.

The recipes in Part Two can form the foundation of a preschool, kindergarten, or family child care cooking program. The recipes are divided into three sections: RECIPES-FOR-ONE, SMALL GROUP RECIPES, and ART AND SCIENCE RECIPES. Before being included, each recipe received the seal of approval from preschool or kindergarten children. Remember, though: Not every child will have the same reaction to a given recipe. For example, one group of preschoolers had a "yuck" reaction to green eggs a la Dr. Seuss; another group of preschoolers declared the same recipe "awesome." So feel free to experiment with these recipes, adapting them to meet your children's tastes and aesthetics. Recipes should be springboards for learning and outlets for creativity.

Above all, have fun. Cooking should be a pleasure, not a chore. Bon appétit!

An ingredient list

Recipes-for-One

Recipes-for-One are intended for each child to prepare individually. If heat or sharp tools are required, an adult needs to carefully supervise the child's activities. In setting up the cooking area for Recipes-for-One, teachers should assume that several children will want to make the same recipe, either successively or at the same time. Therefore, quantities for each listed ingredient should be assembled in bulk for use by multiple children.

Early Morning Fare

Banana Split Breakfast

1 banana
1 (4-oz.) container plain yogurt
½ cup dry cereal
1 handful seedless grapes
1 handful strawberries

knife and cutting board
measuring cup
cereal bowl
spoon

- Peel banana, and slice lengthwise
- Place banana halves in cereal bowl
- Top with yogurt
- Sprinkle with cereal and fruit

Note: Grapes should be cut in half lengthwise for younger children.

Painted Toast

½ cup milk for each color of food
    coloring used
food coloring
2 slices white bread

bowls
measuring cup
pastry brush

- For each color of paint desired, measure ½ cup milk into a bowl
- Add a few drops of food coloring to each bowl
- Paint bread with colored milk
- Toast in toaster oven, painted side up

Dr. Seuss' Green Eggs and Ham

1 egg
1 tbsp. milk
dash of salt
dash of pepper
2-3 drops green food coloring
2 tbsp. butter
1 slice deli ham

mixing bowl
measuring spoons
whisk or eggbeater
frying pan
wooden spoon

◆ Crack egg into mixing bowl
◆ Add milk, salt, pepper, and food coloring
◆ Beat egg mixture
◆ Melt butter in frying pan on medium heat
◆ Pour egg mixture into frying pan
◆ Using wooden spoon, scramble the egg until hard
◆ Remove scrambled egg
◆ Heat ham in same frying pan

PB&J French Toast

2 slices raisin bread
peanut butter (smooth)
jelly
1 egg
1 tbsp. milk
dash of cinnamon
2 tbsp. butter

spreader or butter knife
knife and cutting board
mixing bowl
measuring spoons
whisk or eggbeater
frying pan
spatula

◆ Make a peanut butter and jelly sandwich
◆ Cut sandwich into quarters
◆ Break egg into mixing bowl
◆ Add milk and cinnamon to bowl
◆ Beat egg, milk, and cinnamon together
◆ Dip each quarter of sandwich into egg mixture to coat well
◆ Melt butter in frying pan on medium-high heat
◆ Place each quarter in sizzling butter
◆ When one side browns, turn it over to heat other side

Variations: Use other types of bread. Add bananas, coconut, or other ingredients to the sandwich.

Note: For children with peanut allergies, use cream cheese, cottage cheese, or soft cheese instead of peanut butter.

You Take the Pancake

½ cup all-purpose flour
2 tsp. wheat germ
¼ tsp. baking soda
¼ tsp. baking powder
¼ tsp. salt
1 egg
½ cup buttermilk
1 tbsp. vegetable oil

2 mixing bowls
measuring cups
measuring spoons
wooden spoon
whisk or eggbeater
frying pan
spatula

◆ In one mixing bowl, combine flour, wheat germ, baking soda, baking powder, and salt
◆ Mix with wooden spoon
◆ In another bowl, combine egg, buttermilk, and 1½ tsp. oil
◆ Beat egg mixture
◆ Stir wet ingredients into dry ingredients, mixing with spoon until blended
◆ Pour batter into measuring cup
◆ Coat frying pan with the remaining oil, then heat on medium-high
◆ Pour batter into frying pan to make one large or three small pancakes
◆ When bubbles form on top of pancake, flip over to finish cooking

Egg in a Nest

1 slice bread
1 egg
cooking oil

biscuit cutter or small drinking glass
small bowl
frying pan
spatula

◆ Cut out a circle from center of bread slice (keep circle for another use)
◆ Gently crack egg into small bowl, keeping yolk whole
◆ Coat frying pan with oil, then heat on medium-high
◆ Place slice of bread in pan
◆ When bottom side of bread is browned, flip it over
◆ Pour egg into center of bread hole
◆ Turn down heat to medium and cook until egg is done (about 2–5 minutes)

Power Apple

1 apple
peanut butter (smooth)

corer
spoon or thin spatula
knife and cutting board

- ◆ Wash apple; allow to dry
- ◆ Working around the stem, use corer to remove center of the apple
- ◆ Using spoon or spatula, fill inside of apple with peanut butter
- ◆ Slice apple into peanut butter–filled rings

Variations: Use a ripe pear instead of an apple. Add nuts, raisins, dried fruit bits, or carob bits to the peanut butter.

Note: For children with peanut allergies, use cream cheese, cottage cheese, or soft cheese instead of peanut butter.

No-Sting Honey Bee Snack

½ cup peanut butter (smooth)
1 tbsp. honey
⅓ cup powdered milk
2 tbsp. wheat germ
unsweetened powdered cocoa
　or cinnamon
sliced almonds

measuring cups
measuring spoons
mixing bowl
baking sheet
waxed paper
wooden spoon
toothpicks

- ◆ Mix peanut butter and honey together in mixing bowl
- ◆ Stir in powdered milk and wheat germ
- ◆ Line baking sheet with waxed paper
- ◆ Spoon mixture onto baking sheet, shaping each spoonful of batter into an oval, to look like a bee's body
- ◆ Dip toothpick in cocoa or cinnamon and draw lines across bee's body, pressing to make stripes
- ◆ Stick on almond slices to make wings
- ◆ Chill in refrigerator for 30 minutes

Note: For children with peanut allergies, use cream cheese, cottage cheese, or soft cheese instead of peanut butter.

Cheese Shapies

3-4 slices of cheese

cookie cutters of various shapes
cutting board
plate

◆ Lay out single slice of cheese on cutting board
◆ Using cookie cutter, cut out shaped piece of cheese
◆ Place cheese piece on plate
◆ Repeat using different cutter on each slice of cheese

Variations: Use cheeses of different colors. Use sliced luncheon meat instead of cheese.

Happy Trails Mix

2 cups Chex or other cereal with large pieces
¼ cup dried fruit bits
¼ cup raisins
¼ cup yogurt-covered carob pieces

measuring cups
plastic resealable bag

◆ Empty all ingredients into bag
◆ Close, then shake bag to mix

Variation: Use any combination of dried fruits, nuts, and seeds.
Note: Because of their potential as a choking hazard, raisins should be served only to children who are 4 years old or older.

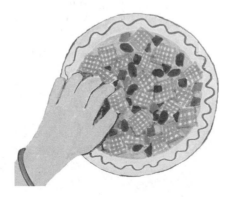

Ants on a Log (or Marching Raisins)

2 stalks celery
1 tbsp. peanut butter (smooth)
10 raisins

measuring spoons
paper towel
spreader or butter knife

◆ Wash and dry celery
◆ Spread peanut butter on celery
◆ Top with raisins

Variations: Use dried cherries or cranberries in place of raisins.

Note: For children with peanut allergies, use cream cheese or cottage cheese instead of peanut butter.

Note: Because of their potential as a choking hazard, raisins and celery should be served only to children who are 4 years old or older.

Fish Swimming Upstream

2 stalks celery
¼ cup cream cheese
8 Goldfish crackers

measuring cup
spreader or butter knife
paper towel

◆ Wash and dry celery
◆ Spread cream cheese on celery
◆ Top with Goldfish crackers, all facing the same direction

Variation: Substitute peanut butter or cottage cheese for cream cheese.

Note: Because of its potential as a choking hazard, celery should be served only to children who are 4 years old or older.

Note: For children with peanut allergies, don't substitute peanut butter in the recipe.

Muchos Nachos

⅛ lb. cheddar cheese
⅛ lb. Monterey jack cheese
small bag of tortilla chips

microwave-safe platter
cheese grater

◆ Spread chips over platter
◆ Grate both cheeses over chips
◆ Microwave for 1 minute or until cheese is melted

Variation: Add salsa, avocado, or sour cream to heated nachos.

Fruity Pizza

1 English muffin
1 slice mozzarella cheese
fruit (apple, banana, pineapple chunks, or seedless grapes)

knife and cutting board

◆ Preheat oven to 400 degrees
◆ Split the English muffin, and toast lightly
◆ Place half of cheese slice on each muffin half
◆ Add sliced fruit to top of cheese
◆ Bake for 10 minutes or until cheese melts

Variations: Substitute a bagel. Substitute dried fruit for fresh.
Note: Grapes should be cut in half lengthwise for younger children.

Skewer Doer

¼ lb. hard cheese, such as cheddar
1 banana
1 bunch seedless grapes
6 strawberries

cutting board and knife
wooden skewers

◆ Cut cheese into cubes
◆ Cut fruit into chunks
◆ Thread fruit and cheese on skewers in any pattern of choice

Variation: Substitute vegetables or luncheon meat cubes.

Note: To prevent choking accidents, this recipe should not be made with children under 4.

Hot Chestnuts

6 chestnuts

knife and cutting board
paper plate

◆ Make an X in the brown shell of each chestnut, using the blade of knife
◆ Place chestnuts in a circle on paper plate
◆ Place in microwave and cook for 1½ minutes at 100% (high) power
◆ Allow chestnuts to cool 2 minutes
◆ Peel off shell to eat

Dippy Eggplant

1 eggplant
garlic powder
salt
pepper
1 strand parsley
½ lemon
1 slice pita bread

fork
baking sheet
potholders
knife and cutting board
spoon
mixing bowl
citrus reamer
masher
measuring spoons

◆ Preheat oven to 300 degrees

◆ Pierce eggplant with fork

◆ Place eggplant on tray, and bake until eggplant collapses (about 30–35 minutes)

◆ Using potholders, move eggplant to cutting board

◆ Let sit until cool to the touch

◆ Slice eggplant in half lengthwise

◆ Using spoon, scoop out eggplant into bowl

◆ Sprinkle two shakes each of garlic powder, salt, and pepper onto eggplant

◆ Using reamer, squeeze 1 tbsp. of lemon juice and add to bowl

◆ Tear pieces of parsley leaves into bowl

◆ Use masher to combine ingredients

◆ Stir mixture

◆ Tear pita into pieces and use to scoop up dip

Note: Only the supervising adult should move the hot eggplant and test its temperature.

You Don't Have to Be a Rocket Scientist Salad

1 lettuce leaf
1 pineapple ring
½ banana
½ cup cottage cheese
3 pitted cherries

plate
knife
measuring cups
spoon

- Place lettuce leaf on plate
- Place pineapple ring on lettuce
- Peel the banana and trim one end so banana can stand upright
- Stand banana inside pineapple ring
- Use spoon to decorate banana with cottage cheese and cherries

One Potato, Two Potato Salad

2 very small red bliss potatoes
½ stalk celery
¼ cup mayonnaise
⅛ tsp. salt
dash of pepper
dash of cinnamon
1 whole nutmeg

knife and cutting board
paper towel
measuring cups
measuring spoons
mixing bowl
nutmeg grater
wooden spoon

- Wash potatoes
- Place potatoes on paper towel in microwave
- Cook at 100% (high) power until tender (about 6 minutes)
- Let potatoes cool until they can be handled
- Cut celery into small slices
- Using knife, cut each potato into small chunks
- Combine potatoes, celery, mayonnaise, cinnamon, salt, and pepper in bowl
- Holding grater over the bowl, grate nutmeg across the grater five times
- Mix well with wooden spoon

Note: Only the supervising adult should move the hot potatoes and test their temperature.

Note: Because of its potential as a choking hazard, celery should be served only to children who are 4 years old or older.

Accordion Tomato

1 large red tomato
1 small ball fresh mozzarella cheese

knife and cutting board
plate

◆ Slice tomato in half (save rest for another recipe)
◆ Place tomato, cut side down, on cutting board
◆ Make four shallow slices in tomato, making sure not to cut all the way through
◆ Cut four slices from the mozzarella ball
◆ Place a slice of cheese in each slit of the tomato
◆ Transfer to plate

Variation: Make your own fresh cheese from the recipe *Homemade Mozzarella Cheese* on pp. 118–9.

Full of Baloney Roll-Ups

2 slices bologna
2 slices individually wrapped cheese

cutting board and knife
toothpicks
plate

◆ Unwrap a slice of cheese
◆ Place a slice of bologna on cheese
◆ Starting at one end, roll up cheese
◆ Cut roll into halves or thirds
◆ Spear each section with a toothpick
◆ Transfer to plate
◆ Repeat with other slices

Variations: Substitute salami, ham, or any sliced luncheon meat for the bologna. Use cheese slices as the outside wrapper. Roll other foods inside, such as whole dill pickle or banana.
Note: Different types of bologna are healthier than others; check nutritional content when choosing foods for children.
Note: Because of its potential as a choking hazard celery should be served only to children who are 4 years old or older.

Cheese-Louise Meatballs

½ lb. ground turkey
¼ tsp. salt
dash of pepper
¼ lb. Swiss cheese
1 egg
¼ cup high-iron cereal (Total, Kix,
    Corn Bran, Product 19)

plastic resealable bag
rolling pin
cheese grater
waxed paper
measuring cup
mixing bowl
measuring spoon
wooden spoon
baking dish

◆ Place cereal in bag and seal
◆ Using rolling pin, roll over bag to crush cereal
◆ Lay waxed paper on counter, and grate ½ cup cheese
◆ Combine all ingredients in a bowl and mix lightly with wooden spoon
◆ Using hands, form mixture into balls (about 4–6 balls)
◆ Place in baking dish
◆ Bake at 400 degrees until brown

Variations: Substitute ground beef. Serve with pasta or rice.

Croc Full of Egg Salad

1 egg
1 tbsp. mayonnaise
dash of salt
1 small whole pickle

medium saucepan
mixing bowl
masher
measuring spoons
wooden spoon
knife and cutting board
plate

◆ Fill saucepan with water and add egg
◆ Boil egg for 15–20 minutes
◆ Drain water, and cover egg with cold water
◆ Let egg sit in saucepan until cool
◆ Remove egg and peel shell
◆ Place peeled egg in bowl and mash
◆ Add mayonnaise and salt, and mix with wooden spoon
◆ Slice pickle lengthwise
◆ Chop half of pickle, and combine with egg mixture
◆ Mound egg salad on plate
◆ Place unused pickle half next to egg salad, skin side up, so it resembles a crocodile

Note: Only the supervising adult should test that the egg is cool.

Ton-a-Tuna Melt

1 can or vacuum-sealed bag of
  tuna fish (packed in water)
3 tbsp. mayonnaise
½ cup alfalfa sprouts
1 slice whole wheat bread
1 slice Muenster cheese

can opener (if tuna is canned)
strainer
mixing bowl
measuring cup
measuring spoons
wooden spoon
baking sheet

◆ Empty tuna into strainer
◆ Place strained tuna in bowl
◆ Add mayonnaise and sprouts, and mix
with wooden spoon
◆ Place bread on baking sheet
◆ Scoop as much tuna mixture onto bread as
will stay on without spilling off
◆ Place cheese on top
◆ Bake at 400 degrees for 10 minutes or until
cheese is melted

Note: Albacore ("white") tuna has a higher
mercury content than canned light tuna, so white
tuna should be avoided with young children.
Note: Alfalfa sprouts should be well washed to
avoid any risk of contamination from *E. coli.* or
other bacteria.

Pita Pizza, Please

1 pita round
1 small jar pizza sauce
¼ lb. mozzarella cheese
1 bunch fresh oregano
1 bunch fresh basil

kitchen shears
baking sheet
cheese grater
waxed paper
mixing bowl
spoon

◆ Using shears, cut out a circle from the top
layer of the pita (removing the circle should
leave just a ½-inch border of pita)
◆ Place pita on tray, with hole facing up
◆ Use shears to cut oregano and basil into
small pieces into bowl
◆ Add half a jar of spaghetti sauce to bowl
and mix well with spoon
◆ Spoon sauce into hole in pita
◆ Lay waxed paper on counter, and grate
cheese over paper
◆ Spread shredded cheese over sauce
◆ Bake at 400 degrees for 15 minutes or until
cheese melts

Variations: Use English muffin or bagel as the
pizza base. Add toppings the children like, such
as mushrooms, pepperoni, pineapple.

Confetti Turkey Salad

¼ lb. cooked turkey
½ yellow bell pepper
½ stalk celery
½ carrot
⅛ cup mayonnaise
⅛ cup dried cranberries

cutting board and knife
mixing bowl
vegetable peeler
measuring cup
rubber spatula

◆ Place turkey on cutting board and cut into cubes
◆ Add turkey to bowl
◆ Slice pepper into strips, then into squares; add to bowl
◆ Slice celery into small pieces; add to bowl
◆ Scrape skin off carrot and slice into small coins, then halve each coin; add to bowl
◆ Add cranberries and mayonnaise
◆ Stir with rubber spatula until mixed

Variations: Substitute chicken or tofu for turkey. Add nuts.
Note: Because of their potential as choking hazards, celery and dried cranberries should be served only to children who are 4 years old or older.

Carrots and Bow Ties

1 cup bow-tie pasta
4 baby carrots (peeled, ready-to-eat)
1 tbsp. butter
1 sprig fresh dill
dash of salt
dash of pepper

large pot
measuring cup
knife and cutting board
plastic pitcher
colander
kitchen shears
wooden spoon

◆ Fill pot two-thirds full with water and heat to boiling on high heat
◆ Place carrots and pasta in pitcher
◆ When water is boiling, pour carrots and pasta into pot
◆ Cook about 9 minutes or until pasta is chewy
◆ Drain carrots and pasta in colander
◆ Add butter to pot while it is still hot
◆ Place pasta and carrots back in pot
◆ Snip dill over pasta
◆ Add salt and pepper
◆ Mix with wooden spoon

Variations: Use penne, macaroni, or other pasta. Grate cheese on top of the hot pasta.

A Tisket, a Biscuit

⅓ cup flour, plus some extra
½ tsp. baking powder
2 tsp. powdered milk
pinch of salt
1 tbsp. oil
1 tbsp. water

measuring cups
measuring spoons
2 mixing bowls
wooden spoon
waxed paper
baking sheet

◆ Combine flour, baking powder, powdered milk, and salt in bowl
◆ Combine oil and water in separate bowl
◆ Add wet ingredients to dry
◆ Mix with wooden spoon
◆ Empty dough onto waxed paper
◆ Flour hands, and form dough into three balls
◆ Place dough balls on baking sheet
◆ Bake at 400 degree for 10–15 minutes

Ham-It-Up Pie

1 slice from can of prepared
    buttermilk biscuit dough
1 slice of ham
⅛ lb. cheese

cheese grater
waxed paper
knife and cutting board
muffin tin
nonstick spray

◆ Lay waxed paper on counter, and grate cheese
◆ Cut ham into small pieces on cutting board
◆ Spray one muffin tin cup with non-stick spray
◆ Place half of biscuit in bottom of sprayed cup
◆ Sprinkle ham and cheese on biscuit
◆ Top with other half of biscuit
◆ Bake at 400 degrees until biscuit is browned (about 8–10 minutes)

Variation: Substitute mushrooms or vegetables for ham or cheese.

Octopus Dog

1 hotdog

medium pot
knife and cutting board
ruler
tongs
plate

◆ Beginning at one end of hotdog, use knife to split vertically, stopping about 1 inch from opposite end (measure to confirm)

◆ Roll hotdog 90 degrees, and beginning at the same end as before, split again, stopping at same place (to yield four "legs")

◆ Into the uncut end of the hotdog (above the legs), use tip of knife to carve a smiling mouth

◆ Above smile, use knife tip to dig out two small holes for eyes

◆ Fill pot two-thirds full with water and heat to boiling on high heat

◆ Put hotdog in boiling water, and boil until legs curl

◆ Remove with tongs, and serve head-up on plate

Variation: Children with good fine-motor skills can split the hotdog three or four times, yielding six or eight legs.

Note: Many brands of hotdogs are not good choices for children because they are high in fat and nitrates; examine nutritional information and choose healthy options.

Note: Hotdogs can be a choking hazard for younger children; this recipe should not be made with children under 4.

Shake It Up, Baby, Yogurt Drink

½ cup milk
½ cup plain yogurt
1 banana
1 handful strawberries
1 handful blueberries

measuring cups
strawberry huller
blender

- ◆ Peel banana
- ◆ Wash strawberries and blueberries
- ◆ Hull strawberries
- ◆ Place fruit in blender
- ◆ Add milk and yogurt
- ◆ Blend

Watermelon Zipper Sipper

1 slice watermelon

cutting board and knife
plastic resealable bag
straw

- ◆ Using knife, cut watermelon away from rind
- ◆ Using fingers, remove seeds
- ◆ Place watermelon in bag and seal
- ◆ Using hands, crush watermelon into juice
- ◆ Unseal bag just enough to insert straw, and reseal around straw

Polar Bear Special

1 cup milk
1 banana
1 strawberry

waxed paper
measuring cups
blender
drinking glass

- ◆ Peel banana halfway
- ◆ Place on waxed paper and freeze for 30 minutes
- ◆ Remove banana from freezer and peel all the way
- ◆ Place frozen banana in blender
- ◆ Add milk and blend
- ◆ Pour into drinking glass; top with strawberry

(Who Says I Never Saw a) Purple Cow?

1 banana
1 cup milk
¼ cup grape juice

measuring cups
knife and cutting board
blender

- ◆ Peel and slice banana
- ◆ Add all ingredients to blender
- ◆ Blend

The Cooking Book

A diet heavy in sugar and fat is certainly not good for children (or for adults!). Many children already eat far too many sugary and fatty foods outside the early childhood setting. So choosing to make a recipe from this category should be only a once-in-a-while thing at most. Some teachers will decide to pass them by altogether.

Ice Cream in a Bag

½ cup whole milk
1 tbsp. sugar
¼ tsp. vanilla
ice cubes
6 tbsp. salt (approximate; may need to add more)

measuring spoons
measuring cups
plastic resealable freezer bags (pint and gallon sizes)

◆ Place milk, sugar, and vanilla in pint bag and seal
◆ Fill gallon bag halfway with ice cubes
◆ Add salt to ice
◆ Place small bag in large bag, on top of ice, and seal large bag
◆ Shake large bag very hard for about 4 minutes or until mixture inside small bag freezes
◆ Open large bag and remove small bag; discard ice

Variation: Add dried fruit, nuts, or granola to ice cream mixture.

Yogurt on a Stick

1 container yogurt (any flavor)
nonstick spray

paper cup
popsicle stick (or tongue depressor)

◆ Lightly spray inside of paper cup with nonstick spray
◆ Fill cup ¾-full with yogurt
◆ Place cup in freezer
◆ After 1 hour, remove cup from freezer and insert stick in yogurt (so the stick is in the middle of the cup)
◆ Return to freezer
◆ When ready to eat, remove from freezer and peel off paper cup

Variation: Substitute fruit juice for yogurt.

Long on Shortcake

1 slice from can of prepared biscuit
   dough
1 small can fruit cocktail
cinnamon
nonstick spray

can opener
spoon
muffin tin

♦ Open and drain can of fruit cocktail
(juice can be saved for another use)
♦ Spray one muffin tin cup with non-
stick spray
♦ Place half of biscuit in bottom of
sprayed cup
♦ Spoon fruit cocktail on top of biscuit
♦ Top with other half of biscuit
♦ Shake cinnamon on top
♦ Bake at 400 degrees until biscuit is
browned (about 8–10 minutes)

Variations: Substitute banana, strawberries,
or other fresh fruit for fruit cocktail.

Underwater Jell-O

1 pkg. blue Jell-O
1 cup boiling water
2 cups ice cubes
handful gummy fish

measuring cups
mixing bowl
wooden spoon
large clear plastic glass

♦ Empty Jell-O package into bowl
♦ Add boiling water to gelatin and stir
with spoon
♦ Add ice cubes
♦ Stir until gelatin starts to thicken
(about 3–5 minutes)
♦ Pour gelatin into plastic glass
♦ Poke 3–4 fish into gelatin
♦ Refrigerate to set (about 30 minutes)

Note: Only the supervising adult should
handle the boiling water.

Apple Dabble

1 apple
10 raisins
1 cup apple juice
½ cup maple syrup
dash of cinnamon
1 whole nutmeg

knife and cutting board
corer or melon baller
small baking dish
measuring cups
mixing bowl
wooden spoon
nutmeg grater
aluminum foil

◆ Cut apple in half, and remove core
◆ Put apple halves in baking dish, peel side down
◆ Place 5 raisins in each scooped-out apple half
◆ In bowl, combine apple juice, maple syrup, and cinnamon
◆ Holding grater over the bowl, grate nutmeg across the grater five times
◆ Mix, and pour mixture over apple halves
◆ Cover pan with foil
◆ Bake at 350 degrees until apples are soft (about 45–50 minutes)

Note: Because of their potential as a choking hazard, raisins should be served only to children who are 4 years old or older.

Small Group Recipes

These Small Group Recipes are intended to be made by four to six children working together with a teacher, an assistant, parent volunteer, or other adult. To keep the activity dynamic, it is very important that groups not get larger than six. Should other children wish to participate in the cooking activity, a new group can be convened in the cooking area to make a second or third batch of the recipe.

It is expected that each small group of chefs will sit down together to feast on the results of their labor.

Early Morning Fare

Mmm Mmm Muesli

1 cup dried apricots
1 cup dried apples
1 cup raisins
1 cup dried cranberries
2 cups rolled oats
½ cup sliced almonds
½ cup shelled pumpkin seeds
¼ cup honey (add more or less to suit taste)
milk or yogurt

cutting board and knife
measuring cups
mixing bowl
wooden spoon
cereal bowls

◆ Chop apples and apricots into small pieces
◆ Add all ingredients to mixing bowl and stir
◆ Serve in bowls, mixed with milk or yogurt

Note: To prevent choking accidents, this recipe should not be made with children under 4.

A Lotta Strata

5 slices bread
3 tbsp. butter (softened)
¼ lb. cheddar cheese
6 eggs
1 cup milk
½ tsp. dry mustard
½ tsp. salt
¼ tsp. pepper

spreader or butter knife
measuring spoons
knife and cutting board
glass baking dish
waxed paper
cheese grater
mixing bowl
whisk or eggbeater

- Preheat oven to 350 degrees
- Thinly spread butter on one side of each slice of bread
- Cut each slice into quarters
- Place bread, butter side down, in pan
- Lay waxed paper on counter, and grate cheese
- Add cheese to pan, covering the bread
- Alternate layers of cheese and bread
- Combine eggs, milk, mustard, salt, and pepper in bowl
- Whisk egg mixture
- Pour into pan, over bread and cheese
- Bake for 45 minutes or until golden and puffed
- Let stand for 10 minutes
- Slice into squares

Variation: Add layer(s) of mushrooms, bell peppers, scallions, or deli ham; sauté in oiled frying pan until soft before adding.

Banana Breakfast Shake

2 bananas
3 cups milk
1 cup cottage cheese
1 tbsp. sugar
1 tsp. vanilla
5–8 ice cubes

measuring cups
measuring spoons
blender

- Peel bananas; break into pieces and place in blender
- Add remaining ingredients to blender
- Blend for 1 minute, until smooth and creamy

Pancake Puff

1 apple
3 eggs
½ cup milk
½ cup flour
¼ tsp. salt
¼ tsp. vanilla
4 tbsp. butter

vegetable peeler
corer
cutting board and knife
mixing bowl
measuring cups
measuring spoons
whisk or eggbeater
frying pan
spatula

◆ Peel and core apple
◆ Cut apple into thick slices
◆ Melt butter in frying pan on medium heat
◆ Add apple pieces and cook 4 minutes, then turn and cook another 4 minutes
◆ Combine eggs, milk, flour, salt, and vanilla in bowl
◆ Whisk egg mixture
◆ Pour egg mixture over apples
◆ Bake at 400 degrees until brown and puffy (about 15 minutes)

Variation: Add ¼ cup dark brown sugar and a dash of cinnamon to the apples in the frying plan; cook until the sugar melts.

Big Deal Oatmeal

2 cups oatmeal
1¾ cups water
4 tbsp. brown sugar
handful pitted prunes
¼ cup milk

measuring cups
measuring spoons
medium saucepan
wooden spoon
knife and cutting board

◆ Heat water to boiling on high heat
◆ Stir in oatmeal using wooden spoon until water is absorbed
◆ Turn off heat
◆ Chop prunes
◆ Stir brown sugar, prunes, and milk into oatmeal

Variations: Add different types of fresh and dried fruit. Omit brown sugar; substitute honey.

Crunchy Carrot and Wriggly Raisin Salad

1 lb. carrots
1 cup raisins
½ cup sour cream (light)
½ cup mayonnaise (light)
1 tbsp. lemon juice
1 tbsp. brown sugar
½ tsp. salt

vegetable peeler
grater
measuring cups
measuring spoons
mixing bowl
whisk or eggbeater
wooden spoon

◆ Peel carrots and grate to measure 4 cups
◆ Combine sour cream, mayonnaise, lemon juice, brown sugar, and salt in bowl
◆ Whisk ingredients in bowl
◆ Stir carrots and raisins into bowl using spoon
◆ Refrigerate before serving

Note: Because of their potential as a choking hazard, raisins should be served only to children who are 4 years old or older.

Neat Cracked Wheat Salad (Taboulleh)

2 cups cracked wheat (bulgur)
2 tomatoes
1 bunch scallions
1 bunch fresh mint
1 bunch fresh parsley
3 lemons
½ cup olive oil
salt
pepper

2 mixing bowls
cutting board and knife
paper towels
strainer
reamer or juicer

◆ Place cracked wheat in bowl and add enough hot water to cover
◆ Let stand for 20 minutes
◆ Chop scallions and tomatoes into bite-size pieces
◆ Wash and dry mint and parsley
◆ Pull leaves from the stems of herbs; discard stems
◆ Place the scallions, tomatoes, and herb leaves in second bowl
◆ Strain the cracked wheat and add to other ingredients
◆ Cut lemons in half
◆ Using reamer, squeeze juice from lemons and add to bowl
◆ Add olive oil and dash of salt and pepper
◆ Mix with spoon
◆ Refrigerate before serving

Dreamy, Creamy Fruit Salad

1 apple
1 cup seedless grapes
1 can (11-oz.) mandarin orange slices
1 can (8-oz.) pineapple chunks
1 container (8-oz.) lemon yogurt

measuring cup
knife and cutting board
mixing bowl
can opener
wooden spoon

- ◆ Cut apple into bite-size pieces, avoiding the core
- ◆ Cut grapes in half lengthwise
- ◆ Add apple and grapes to bowl
- ◆ Open and drain cans of orange and pineapple (juice can be saved for another use)
- ◆ Add orange and pineapple to bowl
- ◆ Add yogurt to bowl
- ◆ Stir with spoon to mix
- ◆ Refrigerate before serving

Variation: Use fresh orange slices instead of mandarin oranges. Add bananas, strawberries, and/or melon balls.

Pick Your Pickle

4 cucumbers (English or pickling, if available)
2 cups rice wine vinegar
4 tbsp. sugar
1 tsp. salt

cutting board and knife
ceramic bowl
plastic wrap
colander

- ◆ Slice cucumbers into coins and place in bowl
- ◆ Add vinegar, sugar, and salt
- ◆ Cover bowl with plastic wrap
- ◆ Refrigerate for 4 hours
- ◆ Drain pickles in colander

Note: A ceramic or glass bowl is necessary as plastic and metal react with the vinegar.

Bag o' (Whole Wheat) Bread

1½ cups whole wheat flour
1 pkg. dry yeast
1 tsp. salt
2 tbsp. honey
2 tbsp. vegetable oil
1 cup hot water
1 cup white flour
nonstick spray

measuring cups
measuring spoons
gallon-size (or largest size available)
  plastic resealable bag
dishtowel
loaf pan

◆ Pour whole wheat flour, yeast, and salt in bag
◆ Seal bag and shake
◆ Open bag and add oil, honey, and water
◆ Seal bag, squeezing out air
◆ Squeeze ingredients to mix
◆ Open bag and add white flour
◆ Seal again and squeeze and knead bag for 10 minutes
◆ Place bag in warm place, such as sunny windowsill or warm stovetop, and cover with dishtowel (to keep dough dark and warm)
◆ Let rise for about 1 hour (dough doubles in size)
◆ Spray loaf pan with nonstick spray
◆ Preheat oven to 350 degrees
◆ Punch dough down through bag
◆ Remove dough from bag and place in pan
◆ Cover pan with dishtowel and set aside
◆ Let dough rise until it reaches top of pan's sides
◆ Place pan in oven and bake until golden (about 35 minutes)
◆ Let bread cool before serving

I Can't Believe It's Butter!

½ pint heavy (whipping) cream
dash of salt

candy thermometer
large jar with lid
strainer
mixing bowl
wooden spoon
saucepan (if cream needs warming)

◆ Let cream stand overnight at room temperature to sour

◆ Measure cream's temperature with thermometer; ideally it should measure about 60 degrees

◆ If below 60 degrees, heat slowly in saucepan; if above 60 degrees, cool in refrigerator

◆ Pour cream into jar until about one-third full

◆ Tighten lid on jar

◆ Shake jar vigorously for 8–10 minutes until clumps form

◆ Pour contents of jar through strainer (liquid can be saved for another use)

◆ Rinse clumps in strainer under cold running water

◆ Transfer clumps to bowl

◆ Add salt

◆ Stir with spoon to mix

◆ Refrigerate until butter is hard

Note: The liquid that separates from the clumps is buttermilk!

Scooped Potatoes

4–6 baking potatoes
1 head broccoli
1 cup bottled cheese sauce
salt
pepper
paprika

fork
cutting board and knife
metal spoon
mixing bowl
measuring cup
wooden spoon
baking sheet

◆ Wash potatoes and pierce with fork
◆ Place potatoes in microwave
◆ Cook at 100% (high) power until tender (about 15–18 minutes)
◆ Let potatoes cool until they can be handled
◆ Cut off top of each potato lengthwise
◆ Scoop potato out of skins using metal spoon and place in bowl; save skins
◆ Add dash of salt and pepper to bowl
◆ Preheat oven to 350 degrees
◆ Cut head of broccoli into small pieces
◆ Add broccoli to bowl
◆ Add cheese sauce to bowl
◆ Stir and mash potato mixture with spoon
◆ Spoon mixture back into potato skins
◆ Sprinkle with paprika
◆ Place potatoes on baking sheet
◆ Bake for 30 minutes
◆ Let cool slightly before serving

Note: Only the supervising adult should move the hot potatoes and test their temperature.

Ooh La La French Bread

3 cups flour (or more if needed)
4 tsp. sugar
1½ tsp. salt
1 pkg. dry yeast
2 tbsp. butter (at room temperature)
1½ cup very hot water
nonstick spray

measuring cups
measuring spoons
large mixing bowl
wooden spoon
candy thermometer
plastic wrap
baking sheet

- ◆ Add flour, sugar, salt, and yeast to large bowl and mix
- ◆ Add butter
- ◆ Using thermometer, test to see that measured water is at 105-115 degrees
- ◆ Add hot water to mixture gradually, stirring all the while
- ◆ Stir for 2 additional minutes
- ◆ If mixture looks sticky, add more flour
- ◆ When dough is smooth, cover bowl tightly with plastic wrap
- ◆ Place bowl in warm place, such as sunny windowsill or warm stovetop
- ◆ Let rise until dough doubles in size
- ◆ Flour hands, and knead dough until smooth
- ◆ Shape dough into one or more loaves or shapes
- ◆ Grease baking sheet with butter, then place dough on sheet
- ◆ Let dough sit for 45 minutes
- ◆ Preheat oven to 400 degrees
- ◆ Bake bread for 10 minutes or until golden brown
- ◆ Let bread cool before serving

A Pocketful of Tofu

½ cup bottled Italian salad dressing
6 mint leaves
1 pkg. (14-oz.) silken tofu
8 scallions
½ cup feta cheese
3 tbsp. vegetable oil
pita rounds

measuring cups
cutting board and knife
mixing bowl
kitchen shears
frying pan
wooden spoon

◆ Chop scallions into coins and place in bowl
◆ Slice tofu into cubes and add to bowl
◆ Pour salad dressing over scallions and tofu and let sit for 20 minutes
◆ Heat oil in frying pan on medium heat
◆ Add tofu and scallions, and sauté until golden brown
◆ Cut pita rounds in half with shears
◆ Fill each pocket with tofu filling
◆ Top with crumbled feta cheese

Mac Snack Attack (with Cheese)

1 lb. elbow macaroni
3 cups milk
12 slices American cheese
12 Ritz crackers
dash of salt
dash of pepper
paprika
nonstick spray

large saucepan
colander
plastic resealable bag
baking dish
metal serving spoon

◆ Place macaroni in saucepan
◆ Cover with water
◆ Boil macaroni until tender (about 8–12 minutes at rolling boil)
◆ Drain macaroni in colander
◆ Preheat oven to 350 degrees
◆ Spray baking dish with nonstick spray
◆ Spoon about one third of macaroni into baking dish
◆ Pour 1 cup milk over macaroni
◆ Lay 4 slices of cheese on top
◆ Repeat layers twice more
◆ Place crackers, salt, and pepper in bag and seal
◆ Using hands, crush crackers and shake bag to mix
◆ Empty bag onto top layer
◆ Sprinkle paprika on top
◆ Bake for 30–40 minutes until bubbly
◆ Cool slightly before serving

Corny Dogs

1 pkg. turkey hotdogs
1 can packaged cornbread twists
6 tbsp. mustard
6 popsicle sticks or wooden skewers

baking dish
cutting board and knife
baking sheet
aluminum foil

♦ Fill baking dish with water
♦ Soak popsicle sticks in water for 20 minutes (so they won't burn in oven)
♦ Cut hotdogs in half crosswise
♦ Split each half lengthwise, but don't cut all the way through
♦ Using knife, fill each split with mustard
♦ Open package of cornbread twists
♦ Roll one slice of cornbread dough around each hotdog half
♦ Cover baking sheet with foil
♦ Preheat oven to 375 degrees
♦ Spear each hotdog with a stick, and place hotdogs on baking sheet
♦ Bake for 30 minutes or until cornbread puffs up
♦ Cool slightly before serving

Note: Hotdogs can be a choking hazard for younger children; this recipe should not be made with children under 4.

Tortilla Chips Ahoy

10 tortillas
salt
chili powder
nonstick spray

cutting board and knife
baking sheet

♦ Cut each tortilla into quarters
♦ Spray baking sheet with nonstick spray
♦ Preheat oven to 325 degrees
♦ Place tortilla pieces on sheet
♦ Sprinkle tortilla pieces with salt and chili powder
♦ Bake for 25 minutes or until crisp
♦ Serve with dip

Meatloaf Muffins

1½ pounds ground beef
1½ cups crispy wheat cereal (squares or flakes)
½ cup ketchup
2 tbsp. brown sugar
1 tsp. mustard
1 tbsp. Worcestershire sauce
1 egg
1 tbsp. milk
1½ tsp. onion powder
¼ tsp. garlic powder
1 tsp. salt
dash of pepper
nonstick spray

measuring cups
measuring spoons
muffin tin (6 cups)
mixing bowl
wooden spoon
small bowl
pastry brush
soupspoon or scoop

- Spray muffin tin with nonstick spray
- Preheat oven to 350 degrees
- In mixing bowl, combine ketchup, brown sugar, and mustard
- Remove ⅓ cup of mixture and place in small bowl
- Add Worcestershire sauce, egg, milk, onion powder, garlic powder, and salt and pepper to mixing bowl
- Mix well with wooden spoon
- Stir in cereal
- Let stand for 5 minutes
- Stir mixture, add ground beef and stir again
- Using hands, divide the meat mixture; place in cups of muffin tin
- Using pastry brush, coat muffin tops with reserved ketchup mixture from small bowl
- Bake for 25 minutes
- If muffins stick, use soupspoon to scoop out

Cheesy Quesadillas

4 tortillas
¼ lb. cheddar cheese

cheese grater
waxed paper
paper plate

- Lay waxed paper on counter, and grate cheese
- Arrange grated cheese on one half of tortilla
- Fold tortilla over cheese
- Arrange more cheese on half of tortilla half
- Fold tortilla over again, so tortilla is now quartered
- Repeat for all tortillas
- Microwave for 1 minute on paper plate or until cheese is melted

Humdinger Hummus

1 (15-oz.) can chickpeas
1 tbsp. olive oil
¼ cup water
1 tbsp. lemon juice
½ tsp. garlic salt
paprika
pita bread or tortilla chips

can opener
blender
measuring spoons
measuring cup
rubber spatula
bowl

- Open and drain can of chickpeas
- Empty chickpeas into blender
- Add olive oil, water, lemon, and garlic salt to blender
- Blend until smooth
- Using spatula, transfer dip into bowl
- Sprinkle with paprika
- Serve with pita bread or tortilla chips

Queen Bean Dip

1 (15-oz.) can black beans
¼ cup water
2 tbsp. lemon juice
½ tsp. garlic powder
½ tsp. ground cumin
dash of salt
dash of pepper
tortilla chips

can opener
mixing bowl
fork
measuring cup
measuring spoons
wooden spoon

- Open and drain can of beans
- Empty beans into bowl
- Mash beans with fork
- Add water, lemon juice, garlic powder, cumin, salt, and pepper
- Mix with wooden spoon
- Serve with tortilla chips

Red Hot Applesauce

4 medium apples
½ cup water
¼ cup sugar
⅛ tsp. cinnamon
1 tbsp. Red Hots cinnamon candies

vegetable peeler
corer
cutting board and knife
medium saucepan
measuring cups
measuring spoons
wooden spoon

◆ Peel and core apples
◆ Cut apples into small chunks and place in saucepan
◆ Add water to saucepan
◆ Cook apples for 15 minutes on medium heat or until tender
◆ Using wooden spoon, stir in sugar, cinnamon, and Red Hots
◆ Keep stirring for 3 minutes or until candies have melted

Tried-and-True Fried Rice

4 cups cooked rice
6 scallions
1 (10-oz.) pkg. frozen green peas
2 eggs
2 tbsp. soy sauce (light)
½ tsp. sugar
dash of salt
dash of pepper
3 tbsp. vegetable oil

knife and cutting board
measuring cup
measuring spoons
small bowl
wok
wooden spoon or cooking chopsticks
whisk

◆ Cut scallions into coins
◆ Break eggs into small bowl
◆ Whisk eggs
◆ Heat oil in wok on medium heat
◆ Add scallions and cook 2 minutes
◆ Add peas and rice
◆ Stir 2 minutes with spoon or chopsticks
◆ Pour eggs over rice
◆ Stir until eggs are cooked
◆ Add soy sauce, sugar, salt, and pepper
◆ Stir to combine

Holy Moley . . . It's Guacamole

2 large avocados (very ripe)
1 scallion
1 tomato
1 tsp. lemon juice
dash of salt
dash of pepper

cutting board and knife
measuring spoons
mixing bowl
wooden spoon

◆ Peel avocados (start with knife, then use fingers)
◆ Chop avocados into small pieces and put in bowl
◆ Chop scallions into small pieces and add to bowl
◆ Chop tomato into small pieces and add to bowl
◆ Add lemon juice, salt, and pepper
◆ Mash and stir mixture with wooden spoon to combine thoroughly

Note: Don't forget to sprout the avocado seed. Use toothpicks to suspend each seed in a jar of water, and watch them grow!

Peter, Peter, Pumpkin-Eater Soup

1 (16-oz.) can solid pack pumpkin, unsweetened
1 tbsp. soy sauce
2 tbsp. honey
1 tsp. garlic salt
½ tsp. powdered ginger
3 cups soy milk

can opener
measuring cup
measuring spoons
large saucepan
whisk
wooden spoon

◆ Empty pumpkin into saucepan
◆ Add remaining ingredients to saucepan
◆ Whisk to combine
◆ Cook on low heat for 20 minutes, stirring occasionally with wooden spoon

Variation: Substitute skim milk if soy milk is not available.

GORP (Good Old Raisins and Peanuts) to Go

1 cup raisins
1 cup peanuts
½ cup sunflower seeds
½ cup pumpkin seeds
1 cup carob chips
1 cup shredded coconut

measuring cups
mixing bowl
wooden spoon

◆ Add all ingredients to bowl
◆ Mix with spoon
◆ Pour into plastic resealable bags . . . and go!

Note: For children with peanut allergies, omit peanuts from the recipe.

Note: To prevent choking accidents, this recipe should not be made with children under 4.

Miss Muffet's Curds (and Whey)

1 qt. whole milk
6 tbsp. lemon juice
salt
pepper
crackers

measuring spoons
measuring cup
large saucepan
wooden spoon
cheesecloth
scissors
colander
2 mixing bowls

◆ Pour milk and lemon juice into saucepan
◆ Cook on low heat until milk starts to curdle, forming clumps (about 5–8 minutes)
◆ Remove from heat and keep stirring with spoon until clumping stops
◆ Cut piece of cheesecloth to line the colander
◆ Wet cheesecloth, wring it out, and place in colander; set colander in sink
◆ Pour curdled milk through cheese-cloth-covered colander
◆ Remove clumps to bowl
◆ Season clumps with salt and pepper
◆ Serve with crackers

Variation: To capture the whey for the children to taste, place the colander in a large mixing bowl instead.

Note: The curdled clumps are the "curds"; the liquid that goes through the colander is the "whey." Adding lemon juice to milk makes it curdle, or become "clabbered." The heat separates the curds from the whey.

Prizeworthy Pretzels

2 (16-oz.) loaves frozen bread dough
1 egg white
1 tsp. water
kosher salt
nonstick spray

ruler
baking sheet
small bowl
whisk
pastry brush
shallow roasting pan

- ◆ Thaw bread dough
- ◆ Divide dough into about 24 pieces
- ◆ Roll each piece into ball
- ◆ Roll each ball into rope, about 12 inches long (measure with ruler)
- ◆ Shape dough into letters, shapes, or traditional pretzels
- ◆ Spray baking sheet with nonstick spray
- ◆ Place pretzel pieces on baking sheet and let stand for 20 minutes
- ◆ Preheat oven to 350 degrees
- ◆ Combine egg white and water in small bowl
- ◆ Whisk egg white mixture
- ◆ Using pastry brush, coat pretzels with egg white mixture
- ◆ Sprinkle pretzels with kosher salt
- ◆ Place baking tray on middle rack in oven
- ◆ Fill roasting pan with 1 inch of water and place on bottom shelf in oven; this steams the pretzels
- ◆ Cook for 20 minutes or until pretzels are golden brown
- ◆ Discard water

Devilishly Good Eggs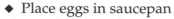

6 eggs
3 tbsp. mayonnaise
1 tbsp. Dijon mustard
dash of salt

measuring spoons
medium saucepan
slotted spoon
colander
knife and cutting board
teaspoon
mixing bowl
fork
rubber spatula

- Place eggs in saucepan
- Cover with cold water
- Add salt to water
- Bring water to boil on high heat
- Lower heat to simmer and cook for 18 minutes
- Pour eggs and water into colander; use slotted spoon to control eggs so they don't break
- Run colander under cold water to stop eggs from cooking further
- Let eggs cool
- Peel shell off eggs
- Using knife, slice each egg in half lengthwise
- Use teaspoon to remove yolks to bowl
- Mash yolks with fork
- Add mayonnaise and mustard
- Stir with fork to mix
- Using teaspoon, place yolk mixture back in egg whites

Note: Only the supervising adult should handle the boiling water and test the temperature of the eggs.

Stone Soup (Like in the Book)

1 clean and sterilized quartz stone

4 cans broth (chicken or vegetable)

2 tbsp. vegetable oil

salt

pepper

Parmesan cheese

1 cup cooked rice

assorted fresh and/or
    frozen vegetables

can opener

cutting board and knife

measuring cup

measuring spoons

frying pan

spatula

large (stock) pot

slotted spoon

bowls

- Place stone in pot
- Slice fresh vegetables
- Add oil to frying pan
- Add fresh vegetables to frying pan, and sauté for 2–3 minutes on medium-high heat using spatula
- Add sautéed vegetables to pot
- Add broth to pot and bring to boil
- Lower soup to simmer
- Add rice and frozen vegetables, and cook until tender
- Use slotted spoon to remove stone
- Allow soup to cool
- Ladle soup into bowls
- Sprinkle cheese over each bowlful of soup

Variations: Vegetables might include any or all of these: potatoes, tomato, celery, carrots, pepper, and zucchini, and medium-size packages of frozen corn, peas, green beans, and lima beans.

Note: Some stones, such as those from a riverbed or bank, explode when heated, which is why quartz should be used.

Note: Only the supervising adult should remove the hot stone from the pot.

Homemade Mozzarella Cheese

Makes 2½–3 pounds of cheese, depending on how long curd drains before shaping

(Time-consuming and complicated, this recipe is best done when
an interested parent volunteer can help.)

3 cups whipping (heavy) cream
1¾ gallons plus 1 cup skim milk
   (29 cups total)
¼ rennet tablet or 1 teaspoon liquid
   rennet
¼ cup cool water
½ cup freshly opened buttermilk
brine (use ½ cup salt for each
   1 quart of water)

3–4 gallon pot
metal spoon
thermometer
small mixing bowl
long knife
slotted spoon
colander
cheesecloth
large pan
plastic wrap
knife
large bowl
large spoon

Before you begin,

◆ Sterilize all tools and containers by pouring boiling water over them or immersing them in boiling water.

◆ During the cheese-making process, have boiling water on hand to pour over tools—spoons and thermometer in particular—each time you return them to the milk mixture. This prevents bacteria from affecting the cheese's flavor.

To make the curd,

◆ Pour cream and milk into pot; stir with a metal spoon to mix

◆ Place pot on low heat until milk mixture reaches 90 degrees, stirring occasionally and checking temperature often

◆ As milk mixture heats, combine rennet tablet and cool water in small bowl; temperature of water should be about 70 degrees. Let rennet mixture stand until tablet is completely dissolved (about 15 minutes); crush tablet with the back of spoon if necessary. Or, if using liquid rennet, mix rennet with water in small bowl

◆ When milk mixture reaches 90 degrees, add buttermilk to pot and stir thoroughly with spoon; remove any lumps

◆ Slowly pour rennet mixture in spiraling pattern over milk mixture, stirring

◆ Continue stirring for 3–5 minutes, using up-down circular motion to distribute rennet evenly in pot

◆ Keep contents of pot at 90 degrees until mixture forms a clot that is firm enough to hold its shape in a spoon (about 30–45 minutes); while waiting for clot, check temperature about every 5 minutes, removing mixture from heat as needed

◆ While clotting, insert thermometer gently to avoid breaking clot apart more than necessary

(continued on p. 119)

Homemade Mozzarella Cheese (continued)

To create crosshatch pattern and to release clear-colored whey,

◆ Cut through solid clot with long knife; knife should cut through to bottom of pot

◆ First cut clot across, then at right angles, for ½-inch squares

◆ Then cut squares diagonally, holding knife at 45-degree angle; turn pot at right angle and repeat

◆ Let curds stand on low heat at 90 degrees for 15 minutes longer (remove pot occasionally, as necessary, to keep temperature from fluctuating)

◆ Stir with slotted spoon for 30 seconds

From this point on, you need clean but not sterilized equipment,

◆ Quickly line colander with at least two layers of cheesecloth, edges overlapping the rim

◆ Set colander in sink with an open drain

◆ Spoon curds into colander; let stand until curds stop dripping (about 1 hour)

◆ To protect cheese's flavor, place colander in large pan; cover airtight with plastic wrap, and chill until curd is ready to shape (about 1–4 days)

◆ Each day, replace cheesecloth and discard any whey that drained out of curds

◆ When curd is ready, divide in four equal portions

◆ Let portions to be used come to room temperature; cover and chill remaining curd in cheesecloth-lined colander until you want to shape it, but no more than 5 days from when you started

To shape cheese, one curd portion at a time,

◆ Trim off and discard any dried-looking bits

◆ Cut curd into ¼-inch-thick slices, and put into large bowl

◆ Pour about 1 quart hot water (170–180 degrees) over slices to cover; let stand 30–60 seconds to warm and begin to melt curd

◆ With back of large spoon, gently push slices together and lift them from beneath, also on spoon back, so weight of cheese makes it stretch. Repeat, lifting cheese along the length to stretch it; don't let rope fold back onto itself

◆ When cheese is flowing softly, lift one end of cheese rope from water and roll it under itself to form smooth-surfaced ball 1–2 inches thick

◆ Pinch ball from rope and drop into brine

◆ Working quickly, repeat to shape rest of cheese; if handled too slowly or roughly, cheese looks uneven—but it's fine to eat

◆ Keep cheese in brine 5–15 minutes to flavor; saltiness of finished cheese depends on length of time in brine

◆ Lift from brine

◆ Repeat to shape remaining cheese

◆ For tenderest texture and most delicate flavor, rinse and serve at once; or keep cold, covered, no more than 4 hours before serving

Note: Rennet is an enzyme that is needed to set milk and form curds. You can purchase either form of rennet online from The New England Cheese Supply Co. at www.cheesemaking.com.

Cider Sipper

4 cups apple cider or juice
4 cloves
2 cinnamon sticks

measuring cup
large saucepan
slotted spoon
mugs

- ◆ Place all ingredients in saucepan
- ◆ Cook on low heat for 5 minutes
- ◆ Remove cloves and cinnamon with slotted spoon
- ◆ Pour into mugs and serve

Lickin' Good Lemonade

6 lemons
1 qt. water
½ cup honey

cutting board and knife
reamer or juicer
measuring cup
pitcher
whisk

- ◆ Roll lemons on counter to loosen juice
- ◆ Cut each lemon in half crosswise
- ◆ Using reamer, squeeze each lemon half to make 1½ cups of juice
- ◆ Pour juice into pitcher
- ◆ Add water and honey
- ◆ Whisk all ingredients

A diet heavy in sugar and fat is certainly not good for children (or for adults!). Many children already eat far too many sugary and fatty foods outside the early childhood setting. So choosing to make a recipe from this category should be only a once-in-a-while thing at most. Some teachers will decide to pass them by altogether.

Oodles-of-Noodles Pudding

1 (12-oz.) pkg. egg noodles
1 stick (½ cup) butter (at room temperature)
1 cup sour cream (light)
1 cup skim milk ricotta cheese (light)
¼ cup sugar
1 tsp. cinnamon
6 eggs
salt
nonstick spray

baking pan (13 x 9 inches)
large saucepan
colander
measuring cups
measuring spoons
knife and cutting board
mixing bowl
wooden spoon
small bowl
whisk or eggbeater
toothpick

◆ Preheat oven to 350 degrees
◆ Spray pan with nonstick spray
◆ Fill saucepan with water
◆ Add several shakes of salt to water
◆ Bring water to boil on high heat, and add noodles
◆ Cook noodles until tender (see package directions for exact cooking time)
◆ Drain cooked noodles in colander over sink
◆ Place noodles in mixing bowl
◆ Cut butter into chunks
◆ Add butter to mixing bowl and stir into noodles
◆ Add sour cream, cheese, sugar, and cinnamon
◆ Mix all ingredients
◆ Break eggs into small bowl, and whisk
◆ Add eggs to noodle mixture
◆ Stir until mixed thoroughly
◆ Transfer noodle mixture to baking pan
◆ Bake for 1 hour
◆ To test doneness, insert toothpick into pudding; if toothpick is clean when pulled out, pudding is done

Variation: This recipe uses a lot of butter; margarine or butter substitute can be used instead.
Note: This dish, also known as *kugel,* is frequently served at Jewish holidays.

Spicy Ricey Pudding

3 eggs
½ cup sugar
1 tsp. vanilla
2 cups cooked rice
1 qt. milk
½ cup raisins
cinnamon
1 whole nutmeg
nonstick spray

measuring cups
measuring spoons
mixing bowl
whisk or eggbeater
wooden spoon
nutmeg grater
aluminum foil
glass baking dish (9 x 11 inches)
roasting pan

◆ Add eggs, sugar, and vanilla to mixing bowl
◆ Whisk to combine
◆ Add rice, milk, and raisins to bowl and mix with wooden spoon
◆ Preheat oven to 350 degrees
◆ Spray baking dish with nonstick spray
◆ Place rice mixture in baking dish
◆ Sprinkle cinnamon over rice
◆ Holding grater over the rice mixture, grate nutmeg across the grater five times
◆ Cover baking dish with aluminum foil
◆ Place baking dish into roasting pan
◆ Pour water into roasting pan so water comes halfway up sides of baking dish; this keeps pudding from cooking too fast and burning on edges
◆ Bake for 1 hour or until golden brown
◆ Let sit for 20 minutes before serving

Yummy-in-the-Tummy Bread Pudding

¾ cup dried cherries or golden raisins
4–6 croissants or brioche
4 eggs
3 cups milk
¾ cup sugar
1 tbsp. vanilla

measuring cups
measuring spoons
glass baking dish (7 x 11 inches)
mixing bowl
whisk or eggbeater or electric mixer
wooden spoon
roasting pan

◆ Scatter cherries or raisins on bottom of baking dish

◆ Tear bread into pieces and scatter over fruit

◆ Add eggs, milk, vanilla, and sugar to mixing bowl

◆ Whisk for 1–2 minutes until frothy

◆ Pour egg mixture over bread

◆ Use wooden spoon to press bread into egg mixture until soaked

◆ Let stand for 15 minutes

◆ Preheat oven to 350 degrees

◆ Cover baking dish with aluminum foil

◆ Place baking dish into roasting pan

◆ Pour water into roasting pan so water comes halfway up sides of baking dish; this keeps pudding from cooking too fast and burning on edges

◆ Bake for 1 hour or until golden and puffy

Note: Because of their potential as choking hazards, dried cherries and raisins should be served only to children who are 4 years old or older.

Flabulous Flan

8 eggs

1 (14-oz.) can sweetened condensed milk

2 tsp. vanilla

1½ cups sugar

measuring cups
measuring spoons
blender
medium saucepan
wooden spoon
cake pan (9-inch round)
roasting pan
toothpick

◆ Add eggs, condensed milk, and vanilla to blender

◆ Blend until smooth

◆ Add sugar to saucepan

◆ Cook sugar on medium heat, stirring constantly with wooden spoon, until sugar crystals melt (Do not let the sugar burn!)

◆ When melted sugar (syrup) starts to turn brown, pour into cake pan

◆ Pour egg mixture into cake pan, on top of syrup

◆ Preheat oven to 300 degrees

◆ Place cake pan into roasting pan

◆ Pour water into roasting pan so water comes halfway up sides of cake pan; this keeps flan from cooking too fast and burning on edges

◆ Bake for 70 minutes

◆ To test doneness, insert toothpick into flan; if toothpick is clean when pulled out, flan is done

◆ Let cool for 1 hour before serving

Note: Only the supervising adult should operate the blender.

Note: Flan is very rich, so portions served to children should be small.

Moony Moon Balls

3½ cups graham crackers
2 cups powdered milk
2 cups raisins or dried cherries
1⅓ cup honey
2 cups peanut butter (smooth)

gallon-size plastic resealable bag
rolling pin
mixing bowl
wooden spoon
baking sheet

◆ Place crackers in bag and seal
◆ Using rolling pin, roll over bag to make crumbs
◆ Add 3 cups crumbs to mixing bowl (save ½ cup crumbs in bag)
◆ Add powdered milk and raisins or cherries to bowl
◆ Mix ingredients with wooden spoon
◆ Add honey and peanut butter
◆ Using hands, mix ingredients together
◆ Shape mixture into balls
◆ Place a few balls in bag with leftover crumbs
◆ Seal bag and shake to coat balls with crumbs
◆ Remove coated balls to baking sheet
◆ Repeat until all balls are covered
◆ Refrigerate 1 hour before serving

Note: Because of their potential as choking hazards, raisins and dried cherries should be served only to children who are 4 years old or older.

Note: For children with peanut allergies, substitute a different recipe.

Banana-on-a-Stick

4–6 bananas
1 cup granola

knife and cutting board
measuring cup
8–12 popsicle sticks (or tongue depressors)
waxed paper
baking sheet

◆ Peel bananas
◆ Cut each banana in half crosswise
◆ Insert stick into flat end of each banana
◆ Pour granola onto sheet of waxed paper
◆ Roll banana in granola, pushing it into banana's surface
◆ Line baking sheet with waxed paper
◆ Place bananas on baking sheet
◆ Repeat for all bananas
◆ Freeze for 2 hours before serving

Chinese Noodle Drops

1 (5-oz.) can chow mein noodles
1 cup carob chips (unsweetened)
½ cup frozen apple juice concentrate
   (defrosted)
¼ cup peanut butter
1 tsp. vanilla

double boiler
measuring cups
measuring spoons
wooden spoon
baking sheet
waxed paper
metal spoon

◆ Place chips, juice, peanut butter, and vanilla into top pot of double boiler
◆ Fill bottom pot of double boiler with water, cover with top pot
◆ Bring water in double boiler to boil on high heat
◆ Cook until chips are melted
◆ Add noodles
◆ Stir using wooden spoon, and re-move from heat
◆ Line baking sheet with waxed paper
◆ Use metal spoon to drop mixture onto baking sheet by spoonfuls
◆ Let harden before serving

Note: For children with peanut allergies, substitute a different recipe.

Art and Science Recipes

As labeled, the ART AND SCIENCE RECIPES are likely to be used in the art and science areas of the classroom. (Because they are not intended to be eaten, they should definitely not be prepared in the cooking area.) The recipes for goop, gak, and the like, have a strong science component. Teachers should also note that recipes in the previous two sections of Part II can underscore science concepts too. For example, in the recipe *I Can't Believe It's Butter!* (p. 105) several ingredients undergo physical changes that children can watch develop. Recipes for art materials lend themselves to cooking in the art area or outside. In small groups, teachers, providers, or parent volunteers can guide children in making paints, clays, playdough, crayons, and chalk.

Chalk

Chalk for the Walk

2 cups plaster of paris
2 tbsp. liquid tempera paint
2 cups water

measuring cups
measuring spoons
baking sheet
waxed paper
duct tape
3–4 empty toilet paper tubes
mixing bowl
wooden spoon

- ◆ Line baking sheet with waxed paper
- ◆ Place pieces of duct tape over one end of each toilet paper tube
- ◆ Set tubes upright on baking sheet, taped ends down
- ◆ Combine all ingredients in bowl and stir
- ◆ Let mixture stand for 3 minutes
- ◆ Pour mixture into tubes
- ◆ Wait until mixture gets firm inside tubes (about 1 hour)
- ◆ Peel away paper tubes
- ◆ Let sticks of chalk dry completely before using (may take several days)

Note: Chalk works well on sidewalks, blacktop, and other hard surfaces.

Walking-on-Eggshells Chalk

eggshells from 5 raw eggs
1 tsp. flour
1 tsp. very hot water
food coloring

paper towels
mortar and pestle
measuring spoons
mixing bowl
wooden spoon

◆ Wash and dry eggshells
◆ Grind eggshells into powder using mortar and pestle
◆ Place flour and water in bowl
◆ Add 1 tbsp. eggshell powder
◆ Add food coloring, and mix with wooden spoon
◆ Shape chalk mixture into a log
◆ Wrap tightly in paper towel
◆ Store in dry place for 3 days or until chalk hardens

Note: Best used on sidewalks. As chalk is used up, peel away the paper toweling to reveal more chalk.

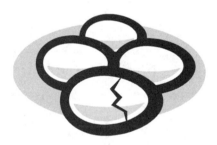

Clever Craft Clay

2 cups baking soda
1 cup cornstarch
1¼ cups water

measuring cups
large saucepan
wooden spoon

♦ Add all ingredients to saucepan
♦ Cook on medium heat, stirring until mixture is consistency of mashed potatoes
♦ Remove from heat and let cool
♦ Knead until smooth
♦ After molding, let clay dry to harden

Variation: Add food coloring during kneading or paint clay when dry.
Note: Only the supervising adult should test the mixture's temperature.
Note: This clay cannot be stored for reuse.

Wake-Up-and-Smell-the-Coffee Clay

¼ cup instant coffee
1½ cups warm water
4 cups flour
1 cup salt

2 mixing bowls
measuring cups
wooden spoon
fork

♦ Place coffee in a bowl
♦ Add water, and stir to dissolve
♦ In second bowl, mix flour and salt
♦ Use spoon to make a hollow in center of flour mixture
♦ Pour coffee into hole
♦ Mix dough
♦ Knead until shiny

Note: After molding, clay can either be stored in a plastic bag for reuse or be hardened by baking in 300-degree oven for 1 hour.

Sun Clay

2 cups salt
1 cup cornstarch
1¼ cups water

measuring cups
medium saucepan
mixing bowl
wooden spoon

◆ Place salt and ¾ cup water in saucepan
◆ Cook on medium heat until salt is dissolved (about 5 minutes)
◆ Remove from heat
◆ Place cornstarch in mixing bowl
◆ Add remaining water to bowl and stir until smooth
◆ Add cornstarch mixture to saucepan
◆ Cook on low heat, stirring until smooth
◆ Let cool before using
◆ After molding, place clay in sunlight to harden; hardened sun clay won't crumble

Note: Only the supervising adult should test the mixture's temperature.
Note: This clay cannot be stored for reuse.

Molding Sand

4 cups fine sand
2 cups cornstarch
4 tsp. cream of tartar
3 cups hot water
vegetable oil

measuring cups
measuring spoons
large saucepan
wooden spoon

◆ Add sand, cornstarch, and cream of tartar to saucepan
◆ Stir in water with wooden spoon
◆ Cook on medium heat
◆ Stir until mixture gets too thick to stir
◆ Let cool before using
◆ Coat hands with oil before molding

Note: Only the supervising adult should test the mixture's temperature.
Note: This clay cannot be stored for reuse.

Recycled Crayons

broken or used crayons

muffin tin
paper (cupcake) liners

◆ Tear wrappers off crayons
◆ Sort crayons by color
◆ Fill muffin tin with liners
◆ Place crayons into muffin tin, a different color in each cup
◆ Preheat oven to 350 degrees
◆ Bake until crayons are melted
◆ Cool
◆ Peel away paper liners

Note: Only the supervising adult should test the crayons' temperature.

Cube Crayons

2 cups Ivory Snow laundry detergent
1 cup water
food coloring
nonstick spray

measuring cups
mixing bowl
wooden spoon
ice cube tray

◆ Place detergent and water in bowl
◆ Stir until creamy
◆ Add food coloring
◆ Spray ice cube tray with nonstick spray
◆ Pour detergent mixture into tray
◆ Let harden overnight before removing

Fabulous Finger Paint I

½ cup cornstarch
2 cups cold water
2 envelopes unflavored gelatin
1 cup powdered laundry detergent
food coloring

medium mixing bowl
measuring cups
wooden spoon
small bowl
medium saucepan
jar with lid

- Place cornstarch in mixing bowl
- Add 1½ cups cold water
- Mix with spoon
- Pour gelatin into small bowl
- Add ½ cup cold water, mix, and let sit for 1–2 minutes
- Pour cornstarch mixture into saucepan
- Add gelatin to saucepan
- Cook on medium heat until thick and glossy
- Stir in detergent
- Add food coloring, and mix

Note: Store on the shelf in an airtight container.

Fabulous Finger Paint II

3 cups water
¼ cup powdered laundry detergent
½ cup liquid laundry starch
food coloring

measuring cups
large saucepan
wooden spoon
eggbeater

- Place detergent in saucepan
- Add water, and stir with spoon
- Mix in starch
- Cook on medium heat
- Stir constantly until mixture turns clear
- Remove from heat
- Add food coloring
- Beat with eggbeater until foamy

Note: Store in the refrigerator in an airtight container.

Face Paint

1 tsp. cornstarch
½ tsp. cold cream
½ tsp. water
food coloring

measuring spoons
mixing bowl
wooden spoon

◆ Place cornstarch and cold cream in bowl and mix
◆ Add water, and stir
◆ Add food coloring, and stir

Note: Paint removes with soap and water. Store on the shelf in an airtight container.

Full Body Paint

1 cup solid shortening (such as Crisco)
2 cups cornstarch
food coloring

measuring cups
mixing bowl
wooden spoon

◆ Add shortening and cornstarch to mixing bowl
◆ Stir
◆ Add food coloring, and stir

Note: Paint removes with soap and water. Store on the shelf in an airtight container.

Move Over Elmer: Make-Your-Own Glue

1½ cups cold water
2 tbsp. corn syrup
1 tsp. white vinegar
½ cup cornstarch

measuring cups
measuring spoons
medium saucepan
mixing bowl
whisk
wooden spoon

◆ Add ¾ cup water, corn syrup, and vinegar to saucepan
◆ Bring to boil on high heat
◆ Reduce heat to simmer
◆ Place ¾ cup cold water in bowl, and whisk in cornstarch
◆ Slowly add cornstarch mixture to saucepan
◆ Stir to mix
◆ Remove from heat
◆ Let glue stand overnight before using

Note: Store on the shelf in an airtight container.

Make Haste with Make-Your-Own Paste

1 cup sugar
1 cup flour
1 qt. water
1 tbsp. cream of tartar
1 drop oil of wintergreen

measuring cups
measuring spoons
microwave-safe mixing bowl
wooden spoon

◆ Add sugar, flour, and water to bowl, and mix
◆ Cook in microwave 2–3 minutes at 100% (high) power or until mixture is thick and clear
◆ Cool
◆ Stir in cream of tartar and wintergreen

Note: Only the supervising adult should test the paste's temperature.
Note: Store on the shelf in an airtight container.

Oobleck (aka Goobleck)

1 cup cornstarch
½ cup water

measuring cups
mixing bowl
wooden spoon

- ◆ Place cornstarch in bowl
- ◆ Pour water on top of cornstarch
- ◆ Mix well
- ◆ Let mixture sit until hard

Note: Oobleck, which comes from Dr. Seuss's *Bartholomew and the Oobleck,* is an unstable substance—a liquid and solid at the same time! Picking up oobleck will make it melt. Throw it in the air, and it will lose its shape and flatten like a pancake. Try making a tubful of oobleck (using the 2:1 ratio of cornstarch to water, but dramatically increasing the quantities) and then encourage children to jump in!

Note: Oobleck cannot be stored or reused.

Great Goop

2 cups water
½ cup cornstarch
food coloring

measuring cups
saucepan
wooden spoon

- ◆ Pour water in saucepan
- ◆ Bring water to boiling on high heat
- ◆ Stir in cornstarch
- ◆ Stir in food coloring
- ◆ Keep stirring until smooth
- ◆ Cool before using

Note: Only the supervising adult should test the mixture's temperature.

Note: Play with goop on a plastic-covered surface. Can be reused; store on the shelf in an airtight container.

Modeling Goop

1¼ cups water
2 cups salt
1 cup cornstarch

measuring cups
saucepan
mixing bowl
wooden spoon

- ◆ Add ¾ cup water and salt to saucepan
- ◆ Cook on medium heat for 5 minutes
- ◆ Combine cornstarch and ½ cup water in bowl
- ◆ Stir
- ◆ Add cornstarch mixture to saucepan
- ◆ Stir on low heat until smooth
- ◆ Cool before using
- ◆ After molding, let sit to harden

Note: Only the supervising adult should test the mixture's temperature.
Note: Can be reused; store on the shelf in an airtight container.

Gak

1 cup liquid starch
1 cup white glue
food coloring

measuring cups
mixing bowl
spoon

- ◆ Pour glue and food coloring into bowl
- ◆ Mix thoroughly
- ◆ Add starch slowly, and mix in
- ◆ Knead

Note: Gak feels like smooth rubber. Can be reused; store on the shelf in an airtight container.

Prime-Time Slime

1 cup liquid starch
2 cups white glue
food coloring

measuring cups
mixing bowl
spoon

◆ Pour glue and food coloring into bowl
◆ Mix thoroughly
◆ Add starch slowly, and mix

Note: Can be reused; store on the shelf in an airtight container.

Very Silly Putty

1 cup white glue
I cup cornstarch

measuring cup
mixing bowl
spoon

◆ Combine ingredients in bowl

Note: Can be reused; store on the shelf in an airtight container. Elmer's Glue-All is recommended; the putty will not bounce or pick up pictures if Elmer's School Glue is used, for example.

Clean Mud

1 bar soap (Dove recommended)
1 roll toilet paper
warm water

large mixing bowl
cheese grater
pitcher

◆ Tear up toilet paper into small pieces and place in bowl
◆ Grate soap into bowl
◆ Mix using hands
◆ Fill pitcher with warm water
◆ Gradually add small amounts of water to bowl, remixing after each addition of water
◆ Mud is ready when it feels like whipped cream

On-Cloud-9 Dough

1 cup water
food coloring
6 cups flour
1 cup vegetable oil

measuring cups
mixing bowl
wooden spoon

- ◆ Place water and food coloring in bowl
- ◆ Add flour and oil
- ◆ Stir
- ◆ Knead until smooth

Variations: In the first step, the food coloring and water can be stirred to mix or the children can drop the food coloring into the water and observe the color spreading.

Note: Can be reused; store in the refrigerator in an airtight container.

EZ Playdough

3 cups flour
1½ cups salt
¼ cup vegetable oil
food coloring

measuring cups
mixing bowl
wooden spoon

- ◆ Mix ingredients in bowl
- ◆ Knead

Note: Can be reused; store on the shelf in an airtight container.

Looks Like Bought Playdough (and Smells Better!)

2 cups water

1 pkg. unsweetened Kool-Aid (purple or orange for intense color)

2 tbsp. vegetable oil

2 cups flour

1 cup salt

4 tsp. cream of tartar

measuring cups

measuring spoons

large microwave-safe mixing bowl

wooden spoon

whisk

large saucepan

◆ Pour water into mixing bowl

◆ Heat water in microwave at 100% (high) power for 1–2 minutes or until boiling

◆ Remove bowl from microwave, and stir in Kool-Aid powder using whisk

◆ Add vegetable oil to Kool-Aid, and stir

◆ Place flour, salt, and cream of tartar in saucepan, and mix

◆ Gradually add Kool-Aid mixture to saucepan, and stir

◆ When smooth, cook on medium heat, stirring constantly with wooden spoon

◆ When dough is done, it will pull away from sides of saucepan

◆ Let dough cool, and remove from saucepan

◆ Knead dough into very smooth ball

Note: Only the supervising adult should remove the bowl from the microwave and test the dough's temperature.

Note: Can be reused; store on the shelf in an airtight container.

Veggie Playdough

1 cup flour
½ cup salt
2 tbsp. vegetable oil
1 cup water
1 tsp. beet, spinach, or carrot juice

measuring cups
measuring spoons
medium saucepan
wooden spoon

- ◆ Combine flour, salt, and oil in saucepan
- ◆ Slowly add water
- ◆ Cook on medium heat until stiff
- ◆ Let cool, and remove from pan
- ◆ Knead dough
- ◆ Add vegetable juice, and knead again

Note: Only the supervising adult should test the dough's temperature.
Note: Can be reused; store in the refrigerator in an airtight container.

Bouncy Playdough

2 cups baking soda
1½ cups water
1 cup cornstarch

measuring cups
medium mixing bowl
fork
medium saucepan
wooden spoon

- ◆ Place ingredients in bowl
- ◆ Mix with fork
- ◆ Place mixture in saucepan
- ◆ Bring to boiling on medium heat
- ◆ Cook, stirring constantly with spoon, until thick
- ◆ Let cool

Note: Only the supervising adult should test the dough's temperature.
Note: Can be reused; store on the shelf in an airtight container.

Basic Bubbles

1 cup dishwashing liquid (Joy or
   Dawn recommended)
2 tbsp. light corn syrup

measuring cup
measuring spoons
container or jar with lid
stirrer

◆ Add ingredients to container
◆ Mix well

Fancy Schmancy Bubbles

1 cup water
2 tbsp. dishwashing liquid (Joy or
   Dawn recommended)
1 tbsp. glycerin
1 tsp. sugar

measuring cup
measuring spoons
container or jar with lid
stirrer

◆ Add ingredients to container
◆ Mix well, making sure sugar
dissolves

Monster Bubbles

6 cups distilled water
¾ cup light corn syrup
2 cups dishwashing liquid (Joy or
   Dawn recommended)

measuring cups
container or jar with lid
stirrer

◆ Add ingredients to container
◆ Mix well
◆ Let sit 4 hours before using

It's for the Birds

1 apple
½ cup raisins
¼ tsp. sand
1½ cups suet
1 cup cooked spaghetti noodles
water

knife and cutting board
cake pan (8 x 8 inches)
meat grinder
bowl
double boiler
tray

- ◆ Dice apple, including skin and seeds
- ◆ Spread apple pieces over bottom of pan
- ◆ Add raisins, sand, and spaghetti to pan
- ◆ With adult's assistance, put suet through meat grinder into bowl
- ◆ Place ground suet into top pot of double boiler
- ◆ Fill bottom pot of double boiler with water, cover with top pot
- ◆ Bring water to boil on high heat
- ◆ Melt suet
- ◆ Remove from heat, and let suet cool and harden slightly
- ◆ Reheat until melted, and pour liquid suet over ingredients in pan
- ◆ Refrigerate pan until mixture hardens
- ◆ Cut mixture into pieces
- ◆ Serve to birds on tray outside

Note: Suet is a fat; the process of *rendering* (melting, hardening, remelting, rehardening) keeps the fat from turning rancid over time.

Recipe Index

References

ADA (American Dietetic Association). 1993. Position of the ADA: Child nutrition series. *Journal of the American Dietetic Association* 93: 334–36.

AOA (American Obesity Association). 2002. AOA Fact sheets: Obesity in youth. Online: www.obesity.org/subs/fastfacts/ obesity_youth.shtml. (See also: Childhood obesity, www.obesity.org/subs/childhood/ prevention.shtml.)

Andersen, G.D. 1993. Clinical nutrition: Cutting boards. *Dynamic Chiropractic* 11 (15). Online: www.chiroweb.com/archives/11/15/05.html.

Barbour, J. 2004. *Children's eating habits in the U.S.: Trends and implications for food marketers.* Rockville, MD: Packaged Facts. Online: www.packagedfacts.com.

Barchers, S.I., & P.J. Rauen. 1997. *Storybook stew: Cooking with books children love.* Golden, CO: Fulcrum.

Barchers, S.I., & P.J. Rauen. 1998. *Holiday storybook stew: Cooking through the year with books kids love.* Golden, CO: Fulcrum.

Basch, C.E., P. Zybert, & S. Shea. 1994. 5-a-day: Dietary behavior of the fruit and vegetable intake of Latino children. *American Journal of Public Health* 84: 814–18.

Bredekamp, S., & C. Copple, eds. 1997. *Developmentally appropriate practice in early childhood programs.* Rev. ed. Washington, DC: NAEYC.

Catron, C.E., & B.C. Parks. 1987. *Cooking up a story: Creative ideas using original stories and props with cooking activities for young children/preschool-k/ages 3-4-5 (flannel board).* Minneapolis, MN: T.S. Denison.

CDC (Centers for Disease Control and Prevention). 2004. *Prevalence of overweight among children and adolescents: United States, 1999–2002.* Online: www.cdc.gov/nchs/products/pubs/pubd/ hestats/overwght99.htm.

Copley, J.V. 2000. *The young child and mathematics.* Washington, DC: NAEYC; Reston, VA: NCTM (National Council of Teachers of Mathematics).

Debord, K., & A.A. Hetzler. 1996, May. *Developmentally appropriate food and nutrition skills for young children.* Pub. no. 348-651. Blacksburg: Virginia Cooperative Extension.

Dickinson, D.K., & P.O. Tabors, eds. 2001. *Beginning literacy and language: Young children learning at home and in school.* Baltimore: Brookes.

Dodge, D.T., & L.J. Colker. 1992. *The creative curriculum for early childhood.* 3rd ed. Washington, DC: Teaching Strategies.

Edwards, C., L. Gandini, & G. Forman, eds. 1998. *The hundred languages of children: The Reggio Emilia approach—Advanced reflections.* 2nd ed. Greenwich, CT: Ablex.

Eneli, I., & P. Crum. 2004. Childhood obesity: Approaching the issue in primary care. *Resident and Staff Physician.* Online: www.residentandstaff.com/ article.cfm?ID=119.

Erikson, E.H. 1950. *Childhood and society.* New York: Norton.

Foote, B.J. 1999. *Cup cooking: Individual child portion picture recipes.* Lake Alfred, FL: Early Educators Press.

Fredericks, L. 1999. *Cooking time is family time: Cooking together, eating together, and spending time together.* New York: William Morrow/HarperCollins.

Gould, P., & J. Sullivan. 1999. *The inclusive early childhood classroom: Easy ways to adapt learning centers for all children.* Beltsville, MD: Gryphon House.

Head Start. 2001, April. Head Start Child Outcomes Framework. *Head Start Bulletin,* no. 70. Online: www.headstartinfo.org/publications/ hsbulletin70/hsb70_15.htm.

Helm, J.H., & S. Beneke, eds. 2003. *The power of projects: Meeting contemporary challenges in early childhood classrooms—Strategies and solutions.* New York: Teachers College Press; Washington, DC: NAEYC.

Kagan, S.L., C. Scott-Little, & V.S. Frelow. 2003. Early learning standards for young children: A survey of the states. *Young Children* 58 (5): 58–64.

Katzen, M., & A. Henderson. 1994. *Pretend soup and other real recipes: A cookbook for preschoolers and up.* Berkeley, CA: Tricycle.

Lind, K.K. 1999. Science in early childhood: Developing and acquiring fundamental concepts and skills. In *Dialogue on early childhood science, mathematics, and technology education: First experiences in science, mathematics, and technology,* ed. American Academy for the Advancement of Science (AAAS). Washington, DC: AAAS.

Lumsden, L.S. 1994. Student motivation to learn. *ERIC Digest,* no. 92. ED 37020.

NAEYC & IRA (International Reading Association). 1998. *Learning to read and write: Developmentally appropriate practices for young children.* Washington, DC: NAEYC.

NCTM (National Council of Teachers of Mathematics). 2000. *Principles and standards for school mathematics*. Reston, VA: Author. Overview online: www.nctm.org/standards/overview.htm.

Ohio State University Extension Service. 1992. *PAUSE With Children. Fact sheet: Parents Appliance Use and Safety Exchange With Children*. AEX-692-92. Columbus, OH: Author.

Parker-Pope, T. 2003. An apple a day: Good eating habits begin at birth. *Wall Street Journal*, 16 December.

Partnership for a Drug-Free America. 2004. Your preschooler. Online: http://health.yahoo.com/health/centers/parenting/71920050.

Rombauer, I. 1931. *The joy of cooking*. St. Louis: Author.

Shonkoff, J.P., & D.A. Phillips, eds. 2000. *From neurons to neighborhoods: The science of early childhood development*. A report of the National Research Council and Institute of Medicine. Washington, DC: National Academy Press.

Snow, C.E. 2000. The theoretical framework and research program of the Home-School Study of Language and Literacy Development. Paper presented at the symposium "Predicting 4th grade reading comprehension in a low-income population: The critical importance of social precursors from home and school during early childhood," chaired by C. Snow, annual meeting of the American Educational Research Association, New Orleans. (For more on the Home-School Study of Language and Literacy Development, see related resources online at www.gse.harvard.edu/~pild/publications.htm.)

Troiano, R.P., K.M. Flegal, R.J. Kuczmarski, S.M. Campbell, & C.L. Johnson. 1995. Overweight prevalence and trends for children and adolescents. The NHANES Surveys 1963–1991. *Archives of Pediatrics and Adult Medicine* 149: 1085–91.

USDA (U.S. Department of Agriculture), Center for Nutrition Policy and Promotion. 1999. *Food guide pyramid for young children: A daily guide for 2- to 6-year-olds*. Washington, DC: Author. Online: www.usda.gov/cnpp/KidsPyra.

Zan, B., R. Edmiaston, & C. Sales. 2002. Cooking transformations. In *Developing constructivist early childhood curriculum: Practical principles and activities*, eds. R. DeVries, B. Zan, C. Hildebrandt, R. Edmiaston, & C. Sales, 121–39. New York: Teachers College Press.

Resources

Children's Literature

Help yourself!—Books with stories about foods, eating, and cooking; others with food-related messages and activities or imaginative possibilities for connection to children's learning and fun with food.

Baby-O. Nancy White Carlstrom. 1992. Boston: Little, Brown.

Blue Moon Soup: A Family Cookbook. Gary Goss. 1999. Boston: Little, Brown.

Blueberries for Sal. Robert McCloskey. 1948 (Reprint 1976). New York: Puffin.

Bon Appetit, Bertie! Joan Knight. 1993 (1st American ed.). London: Dorling Kindersley.

Bread and Jam for Frances. 1993 (Rev. ed.). Russell Hoban. New York: HarperCollins.

Bread, Bread, Bread. Ann Morris. 1993. New York: Mulberry.

Bruno the Baker. Lars Klinting. 1997. New York: Henry Holt and Company.

Bunny Cakes. Rosemary Wells. 2002 (Reprint). New York: Puffin.

Chicken Little. Steven Kellogg. 1985. New York: W. Morrow.

Chicken Soup with Rice. Maurice Sendak. 1991 (Reprint). New York: HarperTrophy.

Cloudy with a Chance of Meatballs. Judi Barrett. 1978. New York: Aladdin.

Dinner at the Panda Palace. Stephanie Calmenson. 1991. New York: HarperCollins.

Dinner from Dirt. Emily Scott and Catherine Duffy. 1998. Salt Lake City: Gibbs Smith.

The Doorbell Rang. Pat Hutchins. 1986. New York: Greenwillow.

Everybody Bakes Bread. Norah Dooley. 1995. Minneapolis, MN: Carolrhoda.

Everybody Cooks Rice. Norah Dooley. 1992. Minneapolis, MN: Carolrhoda.

Family Pictures. Carmen Lomas Garza. 1990. San Francisco: Children's Book Press.

Fannie in the Kitchen: The Whole Story from Soup to Nuts of How Fannie Farmer Invented Recipes with Precise Measurements. Deborah Hopkinson. 2001. New York: Atheneum.

Feast for 10. Cathryn Falwell. 1993. New York: Clarion.

Frank and Ernest. Alexandra Day. 1988. New York: Scholastic.

Frog Goes to Dinner. Mercer Mayer. 1974 (Reprint 2003). New York: Dial.

Gingerbread Baby. Jan Brett. 1999. Itasca, IL: Putnam.

Goody O'Grumpity. Carol Ryrie Brink. 1994. New York: North-South.

The Great Pancake Escape. Paul Many. 2002. New York: Walker and Company.

Green Eggs and Ham. Dr. Seuss (Theodor Geisel). 1960. New York: Beginner Books.

Gregory, the Terrible Eater. Mitchell Sharmat. 1980. New York: Four Winds Press.

Hector the Accordion-Nosed Dog. John Stadler. 1983. Scarsdale, NY: Bradbury.

"Hi, Pizza Man!" Virginia Walter. 1995. New York: Orchard.

The High Rise Glorious Skittle Skat Roarious Sky Pie Angel Food Cake. Nancy Willard. 1996. New York: Voyager.

Hold the Anchovies! A Book about Pizza. Shelley Rotner and Julia Pemberton Hellums. 1996. New York: Orchard.

How Are You Peeling? Saxton Freymann and Joost Elffers. 1999. New York: Arthur. A. Levine.

How My Parents Learned to Eat. Ina R. Friedman. 1984. Boston: Houghton Mifflin.

How Nanita Learned to Make Flan. Campbell Geeslin. 1999. New York: Atheneum.

How Pizza Came to Queens. Dayal Kaur Khalsa. 1995. New York: Crown.

How to Make an Apple Pie and See the World. Marjorie Priceman. 1994. New York: Knopf.

I Need a Lunch Box. Jeannette Caines. 1988. New York: Harper and Row.

I Will Never Not Ever Eat a Tomato. Lauren Child. 2003. Cambridge, MA: Candlewick.

In the Night Kitchen. Maurice Sendak. 1996 (25th Anniversary ed.). New York: HarperCollins.

It's Disgusting—and We Ate It!: True Food Facts from around the World—and throughout History! James Solheim. 1998. New York: Simon and Schuster Books for Young Readers.

Jalapeno Bagels. Natasha Wing. 1996. New York: Atheneum.

The Little Red Hen. Paul Galdone. 1973. New York: Seabury.

The Little Red Hen (Makes a Pizza). Philemon Sturges. 1999. New York: Dutton Children's Books.

The Man Who Played Accordion Music. Tobi Tobias. 1979. New York: Knopf.

Mel's Diner. Marissa Moss. 1994. Mahwah, NJ: BridgeWater Books.

More Spaghetti, I Say! Rita Golden Gelman. 1992. New York: Scholastic.

Mr. Belinsky's Bagels. Ellen Schwartz. 1998. Watertown, MA: Charlesbridge.

Mrs. Biddlebox. Linda Smith. 2002. New York: HarperCollins.

Pancake Dreams. Ingmarie Ahvander. 2002. New York: R and S.

Pancakes for Breakfast. Tomie dePaola. 1978. New York: Harcourt Brace Jovanovich.

The Paper Crane. Molly Bang. 1985. New York: Greenwillow.

Peanut Butter and Jelly: A Play Rhyme. Nadine Bernard Westcott. 1987. New York: E.P. Dutton.

Pete's a Pizza. William Steig. 1998. New York: HarperCollins.

Piggy's Pancake Parlor. David McPhail. 2002. New York: Dutton.

Pizza: A Yummy Pop-Up. Jan Pienkowski. 2002. Cambridge, MA: Candlewick.

Pizza Party. Grace Maccarone. 1994. New York: Cartwheel.

Possum Magic. Mem Fox. 1992 (Reprint). Norwood, S. Australia: Omnibus.

The Princess and the Pizza. Mary Jane Auch and Herm Auch. 2002. New York: Holiday House.

Rain Makes Applesauce. Julian Scheer and Marvin Bileck. 1964. New York: Holiday House.

Sheep Out to Eat. Nancy Shaw. 1992. Boston: Houghton Mifflin.

A Spoon for Every Bite. Joe Hayes. 1999. New York: Orchard.

Stone Soup. Tony Ross. 1987. New York: Dial.

The Stories Julian Tells. Ann Cameron. 1981. New York: Pantheon.

Strega Nona: An Old Tale. Tomie dePaola. 1975. New York: Simon and Schuster.

Sun Bread. Elisa Kleven. 2001. New York: Dutton's.

This Is the Bread I Baked for Ned. Crescent Dragonwagon. 1989. New York: Atheneum.

Thunder Cake. Patricia Polacco. 1990. New York: Philomel.

Tingo Tango Mango Tree. Marcia Vaughan. 1995. Englewood Cliffs, NJ: Silver Burdett.

Too Many Tamales. Gary Soto. 1993. New York: Putnam.

The Unbeatable Bread. Lyn Littlefield Hoopes. 1996. New York: Penguin USA.

Walter the Baker. Eric Carle. 1998. New York: Aladdin.

The Woman Who Flummoxed the Fairies. Heather Forest. 1996. New York: Voyager.

Yoko. Rosemary Wells. 1998. New York: Hyperion Books for Children.

Cookbooks Related to Children's Stories

From a list compiled by Kay E. Vandergrift of Rutgers University, these cookbooks offer recipes connected to stories and characters that children know and love. Her complete list, including cookbooks relating to literature for children of all ages, is available online at www.scils.rutgers.edu/~kvander/ChildrenLit/cookbooks.html.

The Beatrix Potter Country Cookery Book. Margaret Lane. 1981. New York: Warne.

Beni's Family Cookbook for the Jewish Holidays. Jane Breskin Zalben. 1996. New York: Holt.

Clever Cooks: A Concoction of Stories, Charms, Recipes, and Riddles. Ellin Greene, comp. 1973. New York: Lothrop, Lee and Shepard.

Elliot's Extraordinary Cookbook. Christina Bjork. 1990. New York: R7S Books/Farrar, Straus and Giroux.

The Fairy Tale Cookbook. Carol MacGregor. 1982. New York: Macmillan.

The Fairy Tale Cookbook: Fun Recipes for Families to Create and Eat Together. Sandre Moore. 2000. Nashville, TN: Cumberland.

The Frog and Miss Mouse's Wedding. Cynthia Stanton. 1973. London: RHS.

The Great Big Paddington Book. Michael Bond. 1977. Cleveland, OH: Collins/World.

Midsummer Magic: A Garland of Stories, Charms, and Recipes. Ellin Greene, comp. 1977. New York: Lothrop, Lee and Shepard.

The Mother Goose Cookbook: Rhymes and Recipes for the Very Young. Marianna Mayer. 1998. New York: Morrow.

Once Upon a Recipe: Delicious, Healthy Foods for Kids of All Ages. Karen Greene. 1987. New Hope, PA: New Hope.

Pease Porridge Hot: A Mother Goose Cookbook. Lorinda Bryan Cauley. 1977. New York: Putnam.

Peter Rabbit's Cookery Book. Anne Emerson, comp. 1987. London: Warne.

Peter Rabbit's Natural Foods Cookbook. Arnold Dobrini. 1977. New York: Warne.

The Pooh Cook Book. Virginia H. Ellison. 1969. New York: Dutton.

The Storybook Cookbook. Carol MacGregor. 1967. New York: Doubleday.

The Wind in the Willows Country Cookbook. Lady Arabella Boxer. 1983. London: Methuen.

Winnie-the-Pooh's Picnic Cookbook. 1997. New York: Dutton.

Winnie-the-Pooh's Teatime Cookbook. 1993. New York: Dutton.

The Wonderful Wizard of Oz Cookbook. Monica Bayley. 1981. New York: Macmillan.

Wond'rous Fare. Lyn Stallworth. 1988. Chicago, IL: Calico.

Appendix A: Recommended Daily Food Choices for Young Children

Grain Group (bread, cereal, rice, and pasta)

Number of recommended servings: 6

One serving is:

1 slice of bread

½ cup cooked rice or pasta

½ cup cooked cereal (oatmeal, grits)

²/₃ cup ready-to-eat cereal

2–3 graham crackers

3 cups popcorn

2 taco shells

1 tortilla

½ hamburger or hotdog bun

1 pancake

1 small biscuit or muffin

½ English muffin or bagel

9 animal crackers

5–6 whole grain crackers

9 pretzels

Vegetable Group (dark green, leafy vegetables; deep yellow vegetables; dry beans and peas; starchy vegetables)

Number of recommended servings: 3

One serving is:

7–8 raw carrots/celery sticks

1½ cooked carrots

2 cooked broccoli spears

½ cup cooked kale or collard greens

1 ear of corn

1 baked potato

10 French fries

½ cup peas, lima beans, or green beans

½ cup cooked black, kidney, pinto, garbanzo beans, black-eye peas, or split peas

⅓ cucumber

9 snow peas

4 Brussels sprouts

½ cup coleslaw

1 tomato

¾ cup vegetable juice

1 cup raw, leafy vegetables for salad (lettuce or spinach)

1 cup vegetable soup

1 plantain

Fruit Group (including citrus fruits)

Number of recommended servings: 2

One serving is:

1 piece fruit (apple, banana, peach, kiwifruit, orange, pear)

2 apricots

½ mango

¼ papaya

¾ cup 100% citrus juice

½ cup canned fruit or applesauce

¼ cup dried fruit

¼ cantaloupe

⅛ honeydew

½ grapefruit

½ cup watermelon pieces

7 strawberries

12 grapes

11 cherries

Meat Group (meats, poultry, fish, eggs, and nuts)

Number of recommended servings: 2 (total of 5 oz. per day)

One serving is:

2–3 oz. cooked lean meat, poultry, or fish

The following each counts as 1 oz. of meat:

1½ hotdogs

2 slices bologna or other luncheon meat

¼ cup drained canned salmon or tuna

½ cup cooked kidney, pinto, or white beans

½ cup tofu

1 soy burger

1 egg

2 tablespoons of peanut butter

Milk Group (milk, yogurt, and cheese)

Number of recommended servings: 2

One serving is:

1 cup milk, soy milk, or yogurt

2 oz. processed cheese

1½ oz. natural cheese

2 cups cottage cheese

1 cup pudding or frozen yogurt

Fats and Sweets

Eat sparingly, but don't omit entirely

fats: sour cream, cream cheese, vegetable oil, salad dressing, butter, margarine

sweets: sugar, candy, molasses, honey, syrup, soft drinks

Adapted from *Tips for Using the Food Guide Pyramid for Young Children 2 to 6 Years Old*, Program Aid 1647, (Washington, DC: Center for Nutrition Policy and Promotion, U.S. Department of Agriculture, March 1999). Available online at www.usda.gov/cnpp/KidsPyra/PyrBook.pdf.

Appendix B: Five Weeks of Nutritious Morning and Afternoon Snacks

Planning Menu for Morning Snacks

Morning Snack	Monday	Tuesday	Wednesday	Thursday	Friday
Week 1	Apple slices and graham crackers	Cereal and milk	Muffins and juice	Orange slices and toast	Cheese crackers and milk
Week 2	Applesauce and graham crackers	Cheese toast	Muffins and milk	Fruit kabobs and soda crackers	Ants on a log
Week 3	Raisin toast and milk	English muffins with cheese	Fruit and oyster crackers	Cereal and milk	Peaches and wheat crackers
Week 4	Oranges and cinnamon toast	Banana milkshakes	Fruit and cheese kabobs	Graham crackers and milk	Cheese crisps
Week 5	Apple slices and pretzels	Pita bread cheese melts	Cornbread and milk	Raisins and cereal mix	Frozen blueberry waffles and milk

Planning Menu for Afternoon Snacks

Afternoon Snack	Monday	Tuesday	Wednesday	Thursday	Friday
Week 1	Burritos	Vegetables and cheese sticks	Frozen fruit pops and crackers	Milk and graham crackers	Pigs in a blanket
Week 2	Banana milkshake	Peaches and breadsticks	Oranges and pretzels	Rice with milk and cinnamon	Pears and string cheese
Week 3	Pineapple chunks and Hawaiian bread	Yogurt with granola	Cheese crisps	Baked apples and milk	Peanut butter and jelly sandwiches and milk
Week 4	Breadsticks and cheese chunks	Melon wedges and soda crackers	Whole wheat bread with butter and milk	Vegetable sticks and cheese dip	Orange slices with cinnamon graham bears
Week 5	Granola and milk	Pumpkin bread and milk	Banana pudding	Gelatin with fruit and crackers	Apples and cheese crackers